New Library of Pastoral Care
GENERAL EDITOR: DEREK BLOWS

Derek Blows is the Director of the Westminster Pastoral
Foundation and a psychotherapist at University College
Hospital. He is also an honorary canon of Southwark
Cathedral.

Invisible Barriers

Titles in this series

New Library of Pastoral Care
GENERAL EDITOR: DEREK BLOWS

INVISIBLE BARRIERS

*Pastoral Care with Physically
Disabled People*

Jessie van Dongen-Garrad

First published 1983
SPCK
Holy Trinity Church
Marylebone Road
London NW1 4DU

Unless indicated otherwise, biblical quotations in
this publication are from the New English Bible,
second edition © 1970, and are used by
permission of Oxford and Cambridge University
Presses.

The extract from *A Sleep of Prisoners* by
Christopher Fry is reproduced by permission of
Oxford University Press.

Extracts from *Christian Hope* by J. Macquarrie
are reproduced by permission of A. R. Mowbray
& Co.

Extracts from *Stigma: The Experience of Disability* by P. Hunt (ed.) are reproduced by
permission of G. Chapman.

British Library Cataloguing in Publication Data

van Dongen-Garrad, Jessie
    Invisible Barriers: pastoral care with physically
    disabled people. — (New library of pastoral
    care)
    1. Church work with the handicapped
    I. Title   II. Series
    259'.4   BV4460

    ISBN 0-281-04014-1

Filmset by Pioneer
Printed in Great Britain by
the Anchor Press, Tiptree

To the memory of my parents
Barry and Cicely Garrad

and to my husband
Hans van Dongen
for shared commitments and concerns

Contents

―――――

Foreword

The *'New Library of Pastoral Care'* has been planned to meet
the needs of those people concerned with pastoral care,
whether clergy or lay, who seek to improve their knowledge
and skills in this field. Equally, it is hoped that it may prove
useful to those secular helpers who may wish to understand
the role of the pastor.

Pastoral care in every age has drawn from contemporary
secular knowledge to inform its understanding of man and
his various needs and of the ways in which these needs might
be met. Today it is perhaps the secular helping professions of
social work, counselling and psychotherapy, and community
development which have particular contributions to make to
the pastor in his work. Such knowledge does not stand still,
and pastors would have a struggle to keep up with the
endless tide of new developments which pour out from these
and other disciplines, and to sort out which ideas and
practices might be relevant to their particular pastoral needs.
Among present-day ideas, for instance, of particular value
might be an understanding of the social context of the pastoral
task, the dynamics of the helping relationship, the attitudes
and skills as well as factual knowledge which might make for
effective pastoral intervention, and perhaps most significant
of all, the study of particular cases, whether through verbatim
reports of interviews or general case presentation. The
discovery of ways of learning from what one is doing is
becoming increasingly important.

There is always a danger that a pastor who drinks deeply
at the well of a secular discipline may lose his grasp of his
own pastoral identity and become 'just another' social worker
or counsellor. It in no way detracts from the value of these
professions to assert that the role and task of the pastor are
quite unique among the helping professions and deserve to be

clarified and strengthened rather than weakened. The theological commitment of the pastor and the appropriate use of his role will be a recurrent theme of the series. At the same time the pastor cannot afford to work in a vacuum. He needs to be able to communicate and co-operate with those helpers in other disciplines whose work may overlap, without loss of his own unique role. This in turn will mean being able to communicate with them through some understanding of their concepts and language.

Finally, there is a rich variety of styles and approaches in pastoral work within the various religious traditions. No attempt will be made to secure a uniform approach. The 'New Library' will contain the variety, and even, perhaps, occasional eccentricity, which such a title suggests. Some books will be more specifically theological and others more concerned with particular areas of need or practice. It is hoped that all of them will have a usefulness that will reach right across the boundaries of religious denomination.

DEREK BLOWS
Series Editor

Acknowledgements

Many people have contributed to my learning about physically disabled people and so have had a direct or indirect influence on the contents of this book. Foremost among these are the disabled people and their families whom I have known in different hospitals; and the many hundreds of disabled people and non-disabled people who, altruistically, took part in my community health surveys over a number of years.

Several colleagues and friends have given me information, effected introductions, or read and commented on sections of the manuscript at different stages. Help with specific topics is acknowledged in the relevant chapters; while in addition I should particularly like to record my indebtedness to Miss Margaret R. Morgan MBE, Controller of Personal Social Services, The Spastics Society, London; Professor R. A. Parker PH D, B SC, School of Applied Social Studies, the University of Bristol; the Revd Peter W. Speck MA, B SC, Chaplain, the Royal Free Hospital, London; Mr J. Lips, Ministry of Culture, Recreation and Social Work, The Netherlands; and my husband, the Revd J. C. van Dongen D THEOL, formerly of the General Diaconal Board of the Netherlands Reformed Church, where he had national responsibility for the development of the Church's work with disabled people. He has read and discussed the whole manuscript with me, while his cheerful toleration of domestic disruption enabled me to write it.

The responsibility for any errors or misrepresentations in this book remains my own.

The final stages of my research studies in England and the Netherlands were made possible by the award of six months sabbatical leave by the University of Bristol and by a grant from the National Fund for Research into Crippling Diseases, Great Britain.

The human heart can go to the lengths of God,
Cold and dark we may be, but this
Is no winter now. The frozen misery
Of centuries breaks, cracks, begins to move;
The thunder is the thunder of the floes,
The thaw, the flood, the upstart Spring.
Thank God our time is now when wrong
Comes up to face us everywhere,
Never to leave us till we take
The longest stride of soul men ever took.
Affairs are now soul sized.
The enterprise
Is exploration into God.

CHRISTOPHER FRY, *A Sleep of Prisoners*

Introduction

'The Lord does not see as a man sees; men judge by appearances but the Lord judges by the heart' (1 Samuel 16.7).

To write a book about physically disabled people presents the same problems as writing a book about able-bodied people. Given the rich diversity of people, how is it possible to describe the range of life experiences and the range of responses to life that exist among them? To generalize or to summarize (even if it were possible) would result in such inaccuracy as to make the attempt valueless.

As I faced this problem, I thought that I saw a way out of my dilemma. In all aspects of their lives, disabled people and able-bodied people share the same range of feelings, hopes and fears; and they have many of the same life experiences. I therefore decided to concentrate my descriptions on those of the feelings, hopes and fears which are shared but which many able-bodied people expect to be different among disabled people. I would also describe the range of difficulties and differences in the life experiences of disabled people which many able-bodied people either do not expect or do not think about; and I would show how these differences often result in disabled people having a wider and deeper experience of life in some ways, while at the same time they may miss out on some experiences which able-bodied people take for granted.

This book is for people engaged in pastoral care and I deal with the situation outside the pastor, to assist him to understand something of what it is like to be disabled. I also deal with the situation inside the helper, to assist him to understand some of the attitudes and feelings that many able-bodied people have about disabled people, often without realizing it themselves.

1

Physically disabled people are a minority, roughly one-tenth of the population in Britain. The able-bodied nine-tenths therefore have a considerable influence, directly or indirectly, on the lives of disabled people. My conclusions are twofold: that physically disabled people are more vulnerable in many important aspects of their lives than are able-bodied people; and that able-bodied people, by their attitudes and relationships with them, often unwittingly exacerbate this vulnerability. In the following chapters I examine different areas of vulnerability, and I show in what ways the attitudes of able-bodied people may create invisible barriers· which prevent disabled people from sharing an equal place with them in the community. As I see it, a central aim of pastoral care with physically disabled people is to alleviate their vulnerability as far as possible; and, by helping able-bodied people to modify their attitudes and relationships with disabled people, to remove the barriers between them. I aim to provide essential information for use in pastoral care with physically disabled people and their families. I do not give a general description of pastoral care but I look at certain aspects and methods which are particularly relevant to the problems of disabled people and their families.

However, physically disabled people are not a passive minority, dependent on the good will of the majority or of their representatives — the members of the caring professions and voluntary helpers. Disabled people are a diverse and increasingly vocal group who, in recent years, have devised many methods of self-help and developed ways in which they and able-bodied people can co-operate in the community for their mutual benefit. Pastoral care therefore becomes a shared task.

It is these two concepts of vulnerability and reciprocity that I wish to emphasize.

But who are the physically disabled people in a parish? It comes as a surprise to many people to learn that the largest group of disabled men and women in Britain are those who are disabled by chronic bronchitis or other chronic lung diseases. This is not our usual image of a disabled person. We more readily think of people who are paralysed by poliomyelitis, who are spastics, who have had a stroke — all people who cannot walk well, if at all; and we think particularly of people in wheelchairs. This image is encouraged by the use of the international symbol which indicates the availability of services for disabled people—a design representing a person in a wheelchair. But many people are disabled in other less obvious ways, and people with advanced chronic bronchitis can be severely disabled. The following example demonstrates some of the characteristic difficulties and questions which may be encountered by people engaged in pastoral care with disabled people.

Mr Williams, a married man in his early fifties, suffered from severe chronic bronchitis. Any exertion made him so breathless that he needed two hours to get washed and dressed ready for work, leaving home at 7 a.m. each day. He drove his own car to the warehouse where he was employed as a labourer but was quite unable to work when he arrived and had to sit, wheezing, in a corner, while his workmates of similar age covered up for him and did his share of the work. Eventually, the younger men protested to the employer so often that Mr Williams was discharged as medically unfit for work. This was a tremendous blow to him. There was the reduction in his income from wages to national insurance benefits only; but, far more important to him, was the loss of his status as a wage earner. This was accompanied by feelings of resentment against the younger men who had betrayed him, and against his employer who had discharged him. Friends tried to explain that younger people are often less tolerant of older people who become disabled; and they argued that the sympathetic employer could not continue to turn a blind eye when the younger men kept drawing his attention to Mr Williams's increasing disability. Although Mr Williams recognized the force of their arguments, he kept protesting 'But it's how I *feel* that matters'.

A few years later his disease had progressed so far that he could walk only a few steps on the level. He was unable to go out of his house because the change of temperature affected his breathing. So he spent his days, and his nights also, sitting in an upright armchair in the downstairs living-room, with a small table in front of him on which he could lean forward, this being generally the most comfortable position for people with severe lung disease. Normal conversation was impossible for him: he could speak only a few words in short bursts between periods of breathlessness which were somewhat relieved by his use of the oxygen cylinder and mask which stood ready by his side.

What did Mr Williams feel about being disabled? There were times when he recognized that he was partly responsible himself because he had been such a heavy smoker for most of his life; and then he felt guilty that his illness had disrupted family life and caused his wife so much extra work and worry. At other times he kept asking 'Why should this happen to me? Why me?'

The minister of the local Baptist church was in contact with the family through Mrs Williams, and it was important for him to know much more about her husband and the family if his pastoral care was to be relevant and effective. What did Mr Williams really feel about being disabled? How did his physical and financial dependence affect his relations with his wife, his young adult family and his able-bodied neighbours? Did he want to go on living? Was his wife's physical or mental health affected by the situation? Did *she* want him to go on living?

These are the kinds of questions that are encountered in pastoral care with physically disabled people. To try to convey the feel of working with disabled people and their families, I have quoted passages from autobiographical books and essays by disabled people; and I have described several people and families whom I knew well. With two exceptions, the experiences of the people and families described are real, and the conversations took place as recorded. In order to preserve the anonymity and privacy of the individuals concerned, I have changed all the names and, where characteristics might lead to identification, I have either omitted or changed them. In some places I have introduced a few red herrings. The two exceptions are the James and Andrews families, whose experiences are a pastiche of the real experiences of many different people and families. The James and Andrews families as described here do not exist, but what happened to them happens to many people.

When studying the lives and experiences of disabled people, it is important to keep a sense of perspective. In the newspapers we read about divorces and separations, while the happy marriages go unrecorded. Similarly, members of the caring professions tend to have more contact with families who need help than those who do not. In this book I have described some of the difficulties that are experienced by some disabled people; and it is with such people that clergy and others will have most contact in their pastoral care. I have found that work with disabled people and their families is emotionally demanding, but many of the people I came to know have been a source of strength and inspiration to me. There was real reciprocity.

JESSIE VAN DONGEN-GARRAD
Utrecht and Kent
Epiphany 1982

ONE

'Disabled people are people'

(Slogan of the International Year of Disabled People)

―――――――

An example

Mary Hamilton was an only child, born when her parents
were middle-aged. A healthy baby, she grew into a pretty
child with dark hair and large brown eyes. She was a
contented child, but a natural reserve resulted in her being
liked by, rather than popular with, the girls at school. The
boys ignored her. As an adolescent she was somewhat
solitary, and occupied her free time with reading and
needlework. She obtained employment in a high-class
dressmaking establishment, where she did the fine hand-
finishing of dresses to her employer's (and her own) high
standards.

Mary was a healthy teenager, happy at home with her
parents. She found her work interesting and rewarding, and
she enjoyed her hobbies. Health is a difficult concept to
define. The World Health Organisation describes health as a
condition of complete physical, mental and social well-being,
and not merely the absence of disease or infirmity. By this
definition, Mary enjoyed good health.

When Mary was about eighteen, her parents died. She
moved into a small flat in the same neighbourhood and
remained with the same employer. She grieved for her parents,
but her life continued much as before. Shortly after this, she
developed diabetes mellitus and attended the diabetes clinic
of her local hospital. Here she was given a diet to follow, with
instructions how to prepare it, and was taught how to give
herself injections of insulin. She was therefore no longer in
the state of health as defined by the WHO but had developed

a physical impairment which, as it affects an internal organ, the pancreas, is called an internal impairment.

Mary Hamilton developed a physical impairment at the age of twenty which required a change in her usual routine. She needed injections of insulin and she had to prepare a special diet and eat her meals at specified times. However, she was quietly efficient and adapted her life very well. She remained fully independent and active. It is important to recognize this, as there are many people in the community with physical impairments who are equally independent and active.

However, Mary's strict diet and the precise timing of her meals made it difficult for her to accept invitations from friends to have meals in their homes. Limitations of this kind resulting from an impairment are frequently referred to as a social handicap or just as a handicap. Mary got round this difficulty by inviting her friends to her flat for a cup of tea, to do needlework or to listen to records together. Her life continued in this way for the next twenty years.

When she was about forty years old, the diabetes began to affect the retinas of her eyes, and her sight deteriorated. She developed a sensory impairment following her internal impairment. She began to have difficulty at work in doing the fine stitching to the standard required, and she became very anxious that she might eventually be unable to do the work satisfactorily and might be discharged. Her anxiety affected the delicate balance of her diabetic control and she began to have periods of coma. It was no longer possible to hide from her employer the fact of her deteriorating eyesight. However, he was very sympathetic and offered her alternative work which was not so fine and intricate. She accepted this gratefully but she regarded it as demotion and her professional pride was seriously hurt. Concurrently, she experienced increasing difficulty in giving herself her insulin injections; and she became afraid of living alone in case she should go into coma and remain unattended and die. She therefore became dependent on the presence of other people for her safety and for help with her injections. In other words, she had become disabled.

Disability is a limitation in the ability to perform unaided one or more of the essential activities of daily life, which makes some measure of dependence on other people essential.

In Mary's case, this was the inability to carry on her usual work, to give herself the treatment she needed or to be responsible for her own safety.

During this stressful transition period the physician and I, then a social worker, had many discussions with her. We had all known each other for several years so that it was possible for the three of us to work together as a team. The physician outlined the probable course of her disease and warned her that her sight might continue to deteriorate. He and I gave Mary our support and encouragement at this crisis in her life and helped her to express her fears and to find a guideline into the future. It was suggested that she would be wise to train for other work which she could do well as a partially sighted woman and which she could continue if she became blind.

She agreed to go to a residential assessment centre for two to three months to receive guidance about her abilities. At the centre it was shown that her intelligence was high and that her manual dexterity was good: her standard of education was only average but she was quickly able to improve her knowledge of grammar and spelling. She was recommended to train as an audio typist, and this appealed to her.

While at the centre, she discovered that she was popular with both sexes and she was quickly voted onto the social entertainments committee. This personal success, together with the clear recommendation for training for an acceptable job, were a great boost for her morale, so that she embarked on a residential training course in a spirit of optimism and relative self-confidence. As her anxiety subsided, so her diabetic balance became stabilized again and her comas ceased.

On completion of her training, she obtained employment near her flat, in a large office with an understanding head of department. She found someone to share her flat, a woman who helped her prepare her diet and do other household tasks. She was given insulin in tablet form so that she was able to manage her own treatment. In her new employment she worked well, was conscientious and reliable, and was popular with her colleagues and departmental head. Her diabetic balance remained stable and she had no further comas.

In her mid-forties, she began to lose the sense of touch in her finger-tips: she had developed a second sensory impairment. As it remained slight, she was able to continue with typing. Later, when she became blind, she had a guide dog to enable her to go on travelling independently to work and to get around the office building. She was still working for the same employer at the age of fifty.

Discussion

In this example, four concepts have been introduced in addition to the known concept of health: impairment; essential activities of daily living; disability; handicap. Each has been briefly defined. If pastoral care with disabled people is to be effective, it must be related to all aspects of their lives and so it is important that helpers should understand how these concepts apply in the life of each disabled person. The three terms impairment, disability and handicap are used in the sense recommended by the World Health Organisation, and adopted by the World Council of Churches and other international organizations.

Physical impairment

A physical impairment is a disorder in which an organ or limb or other part of the body does not function properly. In diabetes mellitus, special cells in the pancreas do not produce sufficient insulin for the body's needs. This is an example of an internal impairment, because an organ inside the body is affected. In poliomyelitis, one or more limbs may become paralysed; this is a locomotor impairment, as walking or other forms of movement may be affected. When a person's vision deteriorates through the development of a cataract, he has a sensory impairment affecting one of the five senses.

But a physical impairment may also be due to a malformation of part of the body, as with the 'thalidomide babies' whose arms are frequently reduced to small fingers attached to the shoulders. An impairment may also be due to the loss of part of the body, as, for example, when a woman has her womb removed or a young man loses a leg in a motorbike accident.

Multiple impairments

Some people suffer from a psychological impairment which affects their intellectual abilities. The impairment may be a congenital abnormality of the brain such that they are mentally subnormal or have other types of intellectual difficulties which affect learning. Or at any age after birth, a fit person may suffer brain damage, due to a brain tumour, for example, or a head injury or a stroke, which reduces his or her intellectual functioning. Some people may suffer multiple impairments, both a physical impairment and a psychological one. For example, some children suffer multiple congenital impairments: some spastic children are mentally subnormal; children suffering from Down's syndrome (Mongolism) are mentally subnormal and usually have some physical abnormalities also, often structural defects of the heart. When fit people suffer severe brain damage from whatever cause, they become physically disabled and also have some loss of intellectual ability, often with personality changes as well.

Children and adults who suffer multiple impairments present additional problems for pastoral care and for care of all kinds. The intellectual impairments and personality changes create their own special problems and also complicate the problems created by the physical impairments. Therefore, those engaged in pastoral care with people suffering multiple impairments of this nature may find it helpful to supplement their reading with books on mental subnormality and brain damage.

Essential activities of daily living

Most of us only realize the frequency with which we use our thumbs in our everyday lives when we hurt one; then we are painfully aware of every occasion. Similarly, most of us do not realize how many and complex are all the essential activities which we take for granted in our lives until a temporary impairment makes one or more of these activities painful, or difficult, or impossible to perform; or unless we know a disabled person well and appreciate the ways in which the disability affects his or her daily life. These essential activities, which a fit person does without help, may be grouped under four headings: mobility; self-care; domestic tasks; employment. Readers may be interested to work out all the activities in each group, or they may refer to the Appendix to this chapter.

Any person who, by reason of an impairment, cannot perform one or more of the activities which are essential in his life, or who can only do so with help from another person, is disabled. The less he is able to do, the more help he needs. The more help he needs, the more severely disabled he is. So the severity of disability may be expressed in terms of the person's physical dependence on others. This is in direct contrast to the philosophy on which some accident compensation awards, or damages, for disability are made. These are related, not to the loss of functional ability, but to the extent of the physical damage—to the severity of the impairment. It is important to note this difference, as it is often a source of confusion in discussion.

Disability

It has been shown that, except in some legal situations, disability is defined in terms of functional loss and that it is caused by an impairment. The different kinds of impairment result in disability with different characteristics. The most important are described here while fuller details are given in the Appendix.

Acquired disability, of gradual onset. Mary Hamilton was healthy for the first twenty years of her life. Then she developed an impairment which was not disabling and she remained independent for the next twenty years. But her impairments increased in number and severity until she became disabled by them; and she remained disabled for the rest of her life. This is the pattern experienced by the majority of disabled adults: a period of fitness; a period with an impairment; a period in which the impairment causes disability. The duration of these three periods varies very much between different impairments and between different people with the same impairment.

Acquired disability, of sudden onset. A fit person who loses both legs in a road accident develops an impairment and becomes disabled by it almost simultaneously. When a fit person is involved in an accident and receives head injuries of such severity that he or she dies instantaneously, then impairment, disability and death occur at the same time.

Congenital disability. By contrast, a child who is born with severe cerebral palsy has an impairment and is disabled from birth to death. The majority of disabled children in western Europe suffer from congenital, rather than acquired, disability: in the developing countries the majority suffer from acquired disability, mainly through malnutrition.

Handicap

The term handicap is usually used to describe the disadvantages in social life which result from having an impairment or from being disabled. The term social life has a wide connotation, meaning life in the person's society, in the community.

During the 1960s the term handicap was used with the meaning of disability, but it became unpopular with the majority of disabled people and is now less frequently used in that sense. However, some writers still use the terms handicap and disability interchangeably, and the reader should be alert to this source of possible confusion.

Unfortunately, the term handicap is still widely used in relation to mentally subnormal people, who are often referred to, not as people, but by an impersonal collective noun—the mentally handicapped. This is as undesirable as referring to disabled people as 'the' disabled. Hence the slogan of the 1981 International Year of Disabled People: 'Disabled people are people.'

Appendix

Essential activities of daily life

This is an analysis of the essential activities which an able-bodied adult does without help. Children and young people gradually increase the number of their activities according to their ages.

Mobility: walk; climb and go down stairs or steps; get in and out of bed; sit down on and get up from a chair; travel by public transport when required;

Self-care: feed oneself; dress and undress; use the lavatory; attend to menstrual care; wash; shave/put on cosmetics; comb/dress one's hair; clean teeth; trim finger- and toe-nails;

Domestic tasks: shop; prepare and cook food; clean the house; wash, iron and mend clothes and household articles;

Employment: take paid employment outside the home; perform the task as requred; work the full number of hours required—all in accordance with age and sex.

Some able-bodied people, through choice, do not perform some of these activities; this is very different from being unable, through disability, to perform them.

Assessment of severity of disability

A person offering help to a disabled person can make a rough assessment of the severity of the disability by observing or inquiring what the person is able to do unaided; and whether he or she can perform a task easily, with difficulty, only with help or not at all. A few disabled people do not want to be independent and are able to do more than they do. This lack of motivation is an important factor to take into account when giving help.

Characteristics of disability

Disability may have different characteristics, largely due to the differences in the impairments causing disability. The different characteristics have different effects on the life of the disabled person and his or her family.

Disability may be:

congenital as when resulting from cerebral palsy.

acquired, and of sudden onset as when following a road accident.

acquired, and of slow onset due to the progress of the impairment, as in the example of diabetes mellitus.

stable as in the example of the person with amputation of both legs.

progressive due to the progress of the impairment, as in the examples of chronic bronchitis and diabetes mellitus.

fluctuating when the impairment has periods of progression and of remission, as may happen with multiple sclerosis.

visible as with the paralysis resulting from poliomyelitis.

invisible as with the limitation of activity which may result from a heart attack. When able-bodied people cannot see and understand the reason for a person's relative inactivity, they are frequently much less tolerant and helpful than when the cause of the disability is obvious.

These characteristics may appear in different combinations. With cerebral palsy, the disability is congenital and usually visible. Mary Hamilton's disability was acquired, of slow onset, progressive and at first invisible, becoming visible later when people could see that she was blind.

Numbers of physically disabled people

The numbers of adults living in the community who are disabled by physical impairments may be given by making approximations drawn from community health surveys.[1,2] Approximately 7 in every 100 men and approximately 10 in every 100 women are disabled by physical impairments: the proportion is lower in the younger age groups and higher in the older age groups.

Exactly comparable figures for children are not available, but estimates give about 10 in every 100 children as suffering from physical impairments.[3] Some of the children are already disabled by their impairments and others may become disabled if their impairments progress. The large group who have severe speech defects should more properly be described as handicapped, often severely handicapped, in their homes, schools and later employment, rather than disabled.

Principal disabling impairments

Men[1] Among the 7 disabled men in every 100, about 3 are disabled by locomotor impairments, mainly cerebro-vascular disease (e.g. strokes) and arthritic diseases. About 4 are disabled by internal impairments, mainly by chronic bronchitis; while cardio-vascular disease (e.g. heart attack) is the second important impairment in this group. About 1 man in every 1000 is disabled by sensory impairments, mainly defective vision. Deafness is a very severe handicap and the need to rely on others in some cases of total deafness results in disability.

Women[1] The figures for women are somewhat different. Out of the 10 women in every 100 who are disabled by physical impairments, at least 5 are disabled by locomotor impairments. This means that about half of all physically disabled women have a disability which affects walking or other forms of movement. The majority are disabled by arthritic diseases; while cerebro-vascular disease is the second most important impairment in this group, as with the men. About 3 women are disabled by internal impairments; about equal numbers suffer from chronic bronchitis as from cardio-vascular disease. Roughly 6 women in every 1000 are disabled by sensory impairments, mainly defective vision.

Children[3] Again, comparable figures are not available, but children suffering from epilepsy and asthma form two of the larger groups of disabled children.

Note: I have discussed the principal disabling impairments, i.e. those which cause disability in the largest numbers of people. There are also small numbers of children and adults who are disabled by congenital malformations, cerebral palsy, spina bifida and a wide range of neurological disorders. The fact that there are relatively so few people disabled by these impairments increases their difficulties in some ways. Members of the community have less opportunity to learn about their needs and the available health and social services are not always appropriate, because they tend to cater in the first instance for the needs of the larger and better known groups.

It is worth noting that, when we consider disabled men and women together, the largest group of disabled people are those suffering from chronic lung disease, mainly chronic bronchitis.

Notes on the principal disabling impairments

Chronic bronchitis. Chronic bronchitis is caused by irritation leading to damage of the lungs by tobacco smoke and atmospheric pollution (including pollution caused by heavy smoking). It therefore occurs most frequently in cities and industrial areas, and among members of the lower social groups who are more often exposed to industrial atmospheric pollution and who tend to smoke more heavily. The disease is characterized by chronic cough and sputum, and in the later stages by breathlessness and a cyanosed (blue) colouring as the sufferer cannot get enough oxygen through his or her lungs. The disease process is usually complicated by viral or bacterial infection. Eventually the heart becomes affected and the person usually dies from a combination of lung and heart failure, known as pulmonary heart disease.

Arthritic diseases. These are inflammatory or degenerative diseases of the joints.

Osteoarthritis is a degenerative disease of the joints, affecting most often the weight-bearing joints such as the hips or knees. It is seen most frequently in people of late middle age or in the elderly and in people who are much overweight. It occurs occasionally in young people. The disease causes pain in the large joints, and in the small joints it results in pain, stiffness and loss of fine movements.

Rheumatoid arthritis is characterized by symmetrical swelling and stiffness of the joints of the hands and fingers, elbows, shoulders, ankles and knees — usually in that order of frequency. It is painful and leads to deformities of the joints and loss of movement. It may begin at any age but mostly in the twenties and thirties. It is progressive, although the rate of progress varies very much between people. It can be severely disabling.

Rheumatism is the term that people commonly use to refer to pain or stiffness in the joints. About half the people who suffer from some stiffness or pain in one or more joints have no definite diagnosis. The symptoms may be due to a period of over-use or as part of a general infection such as influenza. Mild attacks of rheumatism can usually be relieved by simple medication and seldom cause disability.

Cerebro-vascular disease. This is disease of the blood vessels of the brain. It can lead to a stroke, which can occur in two ways.

Cerebral haemorrhage is bleeding into the brain. The person becomes unconscious and, depending on the severity of the haemorrhage, he or she may die; or make some measure of recovery as described below.

Cerebral thrombosis is the formation of a blood clot in a cerebral artery. The onset of symptoms is usually slower than with a cerebral haemorrhage.

A very slight stroke may lead to no permanent after-effects; but many people survive a more severe stroke with some lasting after-effects. When the damage is to the right side of the brain, the left side of the body develops muscle weakness or paralysis, called hemiplegia. When the damage is in the left side of the brain, there is right-sided hemiplegia. The area of the brain which governs speech is on the left side, so that people with right-sided hemiplegia usually suffer some loss of speech—aphasia. Thus right-handed people with aphasia may also be unable to communicate in writing. There is also sometimes the loss of ability to read words or to understand them. So with a severe stroke that has affected the right side of the body, there may be severe communication and comprehension difficulties. But one should never assume that people are not understanding what is being said to them or in front of them: many of those who have recovered from a severe stroke with loss of speech, have later said what distress and frustration they were caused by being talked about as if they were not there. In addition to some degree of paralysis, and possible aphasia, there may be double incontinence. The distressing situation of a person severely disabled by a stroke

has been graphically described: 'The paralysis creates
dependence on others, the aphasia separates from others and
the incontinence alienates from others.'[4]

Recovery after a stroke varies greatly. Some people return
almost to their former condition, while others may be left
with considerable disability. The outlook now is much better
than formerly, as with physiotherapy many people can be
taught how to use their residual muscle function to the
greatest advantage; and speech therapy can be very effective
with some people. Concurrently, a social worker, or volunteers
working with her, can form a relatives' group for support and
help in the reintegration of the disabled person into the home.

(There is a third form of stroke which is not due to cerebro-
vascular disease. A cerebral embolism occurs when a blood
clot, which has formed in some other part of the body, breaks
away and lodges in an artery of the brain. The effects are
similar to those of cerebral thrombosis.)

Cardio-vascular disease. The chief disease in this group is
coronary artery disease. This is, in principle, the narrowing
of the main artery supplying blood, and thus oxygen, to the
muscles of the heart. Many different factors are thought to
contribute to the onset of this disease but no single cause has
been discovered. The following may be important: diet, lack
of exercise, overweight, high blood pressure, psychological
stress. The disease occurs more often among heavy smokers
than among non-smokers. It seldom occurs in women until
after the menopause. By comparing its frequency in different
countries, research workers have concluded that it is a disease
of prosperity and that its causes are therefore largely social. It
appears in two main forms.

Angina pectoris is a pain felt most often in the middle of
the chest, with clearly defined characteristics, which occurs
when the heart muscle is short of oxygen. When it is felt
during a period of exertion and disappears when the person
rests, it is called angina of effort. If the pain comes on during
either activity or rest and persists for a long time, it is usually
due to severe blocking of a branch of the coronary artery,
resulting in damage to the heart muscle through oxygen
deprivation. The blood clot is called a coronary thrombosis
and the damage to the heart muscle is called myocardial

infarction. This is what is popularly known as a heart attack.

Myocardial infarction is the commonest cause of sudden death among middle-aged people. If the person survives the first few minutes of a severe attack, many medical aids are now available to increase the chances of survival. For this reason, some authorities are offering training in first aid procedures of mouth-to-mouth resuscitation and heart massage.

To suffer a heart attack is a very frightening experience and the person, usually a man, tends to be very cautious about his activity after recovery and his wife is usually overprotective. It is generally considered better for people, physically, and for their morale, to have a level of activity which is just below their maximum, and this can be defined in agreement with the doctor. It has been said that the most important innovation in medical attitudes to people who have suffered a heart attack is the belief that it is better for them to accept reasonable risks.[4]

References in appendix

1 Bennett A. E., Garrad, J., and Halil, T., 'Chronic disease and disability in the community: a prevalence study', in *British Medical Journal*. Vol. 3 (1970), p. 762.
2 Harris, A. I., *Handicapped and Impaired in Great Britain*. Vol. 1, HMSO 1971.
3 Younghusband, E. *et al.* (eds.), *Living with Handicap*. National Bureau for Co-operation in Child Care 1970.
4 Watson, W. C. See below.

Suggestions for reading
Autobiographies by disabled people

Berwick, Lin, *Undefeated.* Epworth Press 1980. Written by a blind, severely spastic young woman who works as a telephone switchboard operator, and who took a course in counselling in order to be of service to others.
Gibbs, Kristine, *Only One Way Up,* Darton, Longman & Todd 1981. An account by a social worker, now in her thirties, of her struggles to survive and to return to work in the community after her second severe stroke at the age of twenty-six; and of the part played by her Christian faith.

Medical and social background

Barnett, C. H., Lumby, H. G., and Taverner, D., *The Human Body*. English

Universities Press 1972. A visual presentation, in diagrams with minimal text, of the structure and function of the body. No previous scientific knowledge is needed to understand it.

Watson, W. C., *Disease and Social Disability.* Collins 1972. Written for social workers by a doctor, it is helpful to other non-medical professional people. 'Social disability' here is equivalent to 'handicap' as used in this book.

TWO

Personal relationships
Variations on a theme

─────────

'Do disabled people make you feel uncomfortable? If so, their greatest handicap could be you and your attitudes' (A British poster for the International Year of Disabled People, 1981).

The feeling of unease which many people experience in the presence of physically disabled people is a complicated response, with numerous causes.

In everyday life there are certain accepted ways of behaving: we usually shake hands when we are introduced; we smile as a response showing pleasure. Some disabled people are unable to shake hands or to smile, and so cannot give these social signals which we know how to interpret and to which we respond automatically. Able-bodied people may therefore have to think out their responses and their momentary hesitation and uncertainty may make them feel uncomfortable or embarrassed. This in turn may make a disabled person feel humiliated, frustrated or angry, or all three. An additional cause of embarrassment for able-bodied people is their uncertainty whether it is appropriate to use the customary greeting of 'How do you do? How are you?'

The following two contrasted examples show the reactions of two recently disabled men to becoming disabled; and the effects of their attitudes and of their relationships with the able-bodied hospital staff. I shall refer to them as Mr Roberts and Mr O'Reilly.

Mr Roberts was a single man, aged forty-four, who normally lived in lodgings. He was a skilled electrician employed by a government department but he had been unfit for work for one year. During that time he had stayed with a widowed cousin in a different county from where he worked. She had cared for him while his undiagnosed illness progressed until he became disabled and confined to a wheelchair. Shortly after his admission to a specialist unit, the diagnosis was made that he was suffering from a very rare disorder causing bone disease and severe, generalized muscle weakness. Appropriate treatment, including physiotherapy, was started and his condition slowly improved. After three months he could walk with the aid of two sticks and attend to his own toilet unassisted except for getting in and out of the bath.

In the ward he did not mix with the other patients and he had no visitors as the hospital was at a considerable distance from his cousin's home and from his work.

During his three months in hospital, I saw him on many occasions. His manner was aggressive and suspicious with all hospital staff and he was resentful because he felt that a year had been wasted before the diagnosis was made and the treatment started. At the same time he objected to physiotherapy and only co-operated grudgingly in his treatment. He had ambivalent feelings about his treatment, both wanting and not wanting it. He was not in any financial difficulty, as he had very considerable savings, but he resented the necessity to draw on them and described to me the many practical difficulties of the previous year. His fear, anger and resentment were apparent in everything he said. However, he was not able openly to recognize these emotions or to talk about them.

I did not know what his personality had been before he became disabled, but I had the impression of a morose, lonely man, with little self-confidence. This had been further undermined by the frightening experience of becoming steadily more disabled while no doctor could say why or could arrest the process.

A stereotype of the medical profession, which is still held by many people, is that doctors are all-knowing and powerful: when you feel ill you go to a doctor and he makes you well. Mr Roberts's experience with the series of doctors to whom he had been referred during the previous year showed him that his beliefs about doctors were wrong in every particular, and he bitterly resented their failure to live up to his initial expectations. He arrived in the ward strongly prejudiced against all doctors and, by association, all related professions. He therefore expected the worst.

When his disorder was diagnosed within a short time, and when he started to improve as soon as he began treatment, the emotional shock was almost as great as the earlier shock of disability. He could not believe it. During the previous year, he had begun to look upon himself as a disabled person. Because he prized activity, occupation and wage earning, he considered disability to be a stigma. The term stigma was originally applied to the branding on the body of a Greek slave or other 'undesirable' category of individual, but gradually it came to be applied to the disgrace itself, rather than to the evidence for it. The word is now frequently used for any characteristic which appears to set someone apart from others. Mr Roberts had begun to devalue himself. His self-image had changed, and, because his values remained unaltered, he despised the man he now felt himself to be. His self-image fell far below his ideal self-image. As a result, he assumed that other people despised him too; he projected his own feelings onto other people.

This notion of the self-image is based partly on the concepts of 'I', 'me' and 'the self', and also on the body-image, a term which refers to a person's perceptions of his physical body. These perceptions are normally acquired in infancy through physical exploration of the body and are modified and elaborated during physical and emotional maturation. The congenitally disabled child who is unable to explore his body has an incomplete body-image, so that his self-image is deficient in an important component. The person who becomes disabled later in life has to develop a new body-image; while his new self-image will depend partly on that, it will also be influenced by the value that he attaches to able-bodiedness, and by his previous attitudes to disability and disabled people generally. The other components of every person's self-image are developed from his knowledge of himself as a person which he gains in his relationships with other people, and from his perceptions of other people's assessments of him as a person. But each person has his ideal self-image (how he would like to be) and his ideal body-image (how he would like to look) which are based directly on his value-system. A person's evaluation of himself depends on how closely his self-image and body-image approximate to his ideal self- and body-image.

When Mr Roberts began to make a good physical recovery, he found it hard to make a second adjustment of his self-image, and to think of himself as a man in transition from being disabled to one becoming able-bodied again. His prejudice against the medical staff and others made him cynical and he did not really believe their assurances that he would recover completely and not relapse. When a person has been very ill and makes a good physical recovery, there is often a delay before the emotional recovery. Frequently, people feel that they are still ill when they are convalescent and convalescent when they are physically well. This is not malingering but is due to a delay in emotional adjustment, largely as a result of the time that it usually takes to develop a changed self-image.

I encouraged Mr Roberts to talk openly about his evident anxieties about his health — past, present and future — in the hope that I might be able to allay some of his fears. But he was not able to discuss his feelings apart from that of resentment towards the medical profession. When a diagnosis was made, treatment was started and recovery began, his apparent attitude was not one of relief — 'At last!' — but rather, 'If these men can do it, why couldn't all the others? Why the wasted year?' He could not accept that, as his disease was rare, most doctors would never have met a patient suffering from it.

The physician recommended that Mr Roberts should go to a residential medical rehabilitation centre where his increasing abilities could be restored to full working capacity. He would then be able to resume his former employment, as his job had been kept open for him. He listened to my description of the centre and, without enthusiasm, agreed to go there. At the centre he complained continually of being overworked; and the social worker there experienced the same difficulties of communication with him.

After three months at the centre, he was able to resume his former skilled work to the same standard as before. When he attended the hospital follow-up clinic after he had been back at work for three months (i.e. nine months after his admission to hospital) his attitude appeared to be unchanged. I had the impression that his one year of progressive illness, followed by six months of successful treatment, had been two successive crises of such major proportions that he was not able to make a full readjustment afterwards.

Mr O'Reilly was a married man, aged forty-nine who worked as a skilled machine-tool fitter in a large industrial concern. He had suffered from very high blood pressure, and a few weeks before his admission to hospital he had had a blood clot in an artery of the spine. This resulted in partial paralysis of both legs (paraplegia), occasional double incontinence, and impotence. He was admitted to the ward in this condition for confirmation of diagnosis and for treatment. He received treatment for his high blood pressure, started a programme of physiotherapy to improve his muscle function as far as possible, and was fitted with appropriate appliances for his incontinence. The fact of his impotence was merely recorded in the medical notes.

After a month of treatment, his condition was very slightly improved. It was recommended that he should go to the same rehabilitation centre as Mr Roberts, where he would be able to continue his mobilization treatment, and an assessment would be made of his residual abilities. In the sheltered conditions of the centre he would be able to learn new methods of managing the activities of daily living in order to be as independent as possible, and to begin to live with the physical disability from which he would not recover completely.

At this point I was told about him by the physician and was asked to see him. Mr O'Reilly was sitting up in bed, reading a newspaper. I introduced myself and offered him the opportunity to talk about any aspects of his illness that he wished. This opened the flood-gates. In an angry tirade of polysyllabic words, he described his feelings about his disability and made an adverse comparison between what he thought were the attitudes of the medical staff and others towards him and what he thought they ought to be. He was bitter that he had become disabled and that the staff appeared to accept it 'all in the day's work' without considering what it meant to him. He was convinced that, by recommending him to go to the rehabilitation centre, they were throwing him out as incurable. He was so angry that he would have hit me if he could.

I suggested that we should have a detailed discussion of each of these points in turn, and I asked his permission to make notes for the personal records which were kept separately from the medical ones. This clear demonstration that a member of the staff was prepared to listen and to pay full attention to what he had to say, reduced the emotional tension and his anger slowly subsided. It was then possible to discuss the treatment policy in general and how it applied to him in particular. During our discussion he realized that most of his anger at becoming disabled had been redirected onto the medical staff and others. His prejudice against them had then resulted in selective perception, so that he had interpreted all their actions in the light of his negative attitudes. Selective perception occurs when, for example, adverse prejudice blinds someone to the good characteristics of another person: only the bad is seen and every action is interpreted in an adverse way. Similarly, positive prejudice may result in selective perception in the other direction, making someone see another individual through rose-coloured spectacles.

When these misunderstandings had been sorted out, Mr O'Reilly was able to say that his anger towards the medical staff had been exacerbated by his feelings of deep humiliation at being doubly incontinent, a condition that the medical staff could not cure. At this stage he did not mention his impotence and I took my cue from him and did not raise the subject, as he was clearly not ready to talk about it.

After this lengthy discussion he became more positive and described his intention of benefiting from any treatment available. He also outlined his hopes for the future within the limits of his disability. In other words, he had strong motivation to benefit fully from the treatment in order to be as independent as possible. He asked me to see him again after he had talked over the proposed treatment plans with his wife.

In our second conversation, Mr O'Reilly agreed to go to the rehabilitation centre but asked to be allowed to go home to his wife while he was waiting for the vacancy. He talked about their good relationship and raised the topic of his impotence, describing how they had started to make some readjustments before his admission to hospital. He asked me to talk with his wife also.

Mrs O'Reilly had a clerical post in a large administrative organization. She talked easily and covered much the same ground as her husband. At the end of our discussion she said, 'Now I know where I am.'

My third talk with Mr O'Reilly dealt largely with the administrative arrangements for his admission to the centre and with plans for obtaining suitable employment when both the severity of his residual disability and his ability were known.

When these findings had been summarized for the medical staff, it was agreed that he should be referred to a physician who specialized in the social rehabilitation of people with spinal injuries, for help with emotional and practical difficulties arising from his impotence.

On the morning of his discharge from the hospital, Mr O'Reilly apologized to me for what he referred to as his earlier rudeness and anger, saying it was clear to him I would understand that a newly disabled man would react in that way. He thought that the medical staff probably understood too, but 'they do not let the patients see it'.

During our three conversations, Mr O'Reilly had also talked about his interest in politics, economics and theology; he said that his reading 'ranged from Voltaire to the Confessions of St Augustine'. He was a man with considerable verbal facility and was well able to conceptualize. Because he had a great deal of self-insight and was in touch with his own feelings, these feelings could be talked about without the danger that he would intellectualize them and so remove the emotional component from the discussion. Therefore he was able to change his attitude considerably in the course of only a few days—towards the staff, his treatment, himself. He accepted himself as a person: disabled, yes; changed in some ways, yes; but still a person of worth. It has been shown that the person who regards him- or herself in this way makes the best use of rehabilitation facilities and the best readjustment to pursuing as active a life as possible as a disabled person. In other words, the newly disabled person whose revised self-image is of a somewhat different but still valuable person, makes a better readjustment in the family and in the community than one whose self-image is of a changed person of lowered value.

He or she also does better than those disabled people who have an unrealistically high assessment of themselves. Such a self-assessment, involving an unrealistic attitude, may result in the person's attempting tasks or trying to cope with a range of situations which are quite beyond his or her actual abilities. Such people have an unrealistically high level of aspiration. This usually leads to repeated failures, when their level of attainment does not match up to their aspiration. Sometimes their attainment is good, but, because it is not good enough for them, they regard themselves as failures. This may result in depression, frustration and anger. In the long run, the person may then devalue him- or herself excessively.

One task of those helping disabled people who have these particular difficulties, is to help them to obtain a realistic self-assessment as early as possible. This is one of the great values of the Family Assessment Centres which are run by some voluntary organizations. Here a range of specialists (medical, psychological, social, educational, occupational) can help the individual, the family members separately and the family as a unit, to make a good assessment of their strengths and weaknesses.

Readers may feel that, in the description of these two men, Mr O'Reilly comes over more clearly as a person than Mr Roberts. This is because I made contact with Mr O'Reilly: we really met each other as people in a personal relationship. Mr Roberts held me off: he created a barrier by dwelling on his resentments, so that we did not establish a relationship. A university colleague used to say 'Two eggs cannot interact', and, by drawing two ovals on the blackboard, would show the impossibility of two smooth surfaces interlocking. It is only when both people in a pair take some risk and expose their feelings to some extent, that there is any chance of their interlocking and establishing a personal relationship.

The relationship between a disabled person and an able-bodied person may sometimes be adversely influenced by one or more of the following: by lack of, or misinterpretation of, social signals; by the use of stereotypes; by selective perception. It can be profoundly influenced by attitudes and values including the belief that disability is a stigma, and by the self-image and self-evaluation that each person has. Both people must share the responsibility for the success or failure of a relationship: sometimes the greater share of the responsibility falls on the one, sometimes on the other.

Mr Roberts and Mr O'Reilly were both middle-aged men with nearly fifty years of life experience behind them, so they were · to some extent the product of their upbringing, environment and experiences. All these factors influenced the way in which they coped with the crisis of becoming disabled. It is therefore helpful to look at the patterns of relationships within a family and a community which have a formative influence on a child and an adult, and at the different experience of able-bodied people and many disabled people.

The family life-cycle

Mr and Mrs James were an independent, able-bodied couple who had their first child, Philip. He was a healthy baby but initially he required total care from his parents. Before his birth, his parents were primarily concerned with each other but on his arrival they opened their relationship to include him. In so doing, their relationship was changed in subtle ways as they ceased to be husband and wife and became husband-and-father and wife-and-mother. At different times their marital relationship predominated and at others their parental relationship. Sometimes one or other of the adults experienced tension in his or her role in the family, a feeling of being pulled two ways. Sometimes the woman wanted to be wife when the child required her to be mother; or the man, feeling husband, wanted her to be wife when she was feeling mother to the child. However, the couple found a way to resolve these tensions and family harmony, integration and unity were maintained.

As the boy grew up, he became increasingly independent of his parents, first physically and then emotionally. Eventually, he met an able-bodied, independent girl; they married and he left the parental home. His parents then resumed a primarily husband-and-wife relationship. In late middle age Mrs James developed an arthritic impairment which progressed. She became slightly disabled and partly dependent on her husband. Subsequently he had a severe heart attack, from which he died. Mrs James was then partly dependent on her son and daughter-in-law.

In these two generations, we see, first, that the family life-cycle is one from dependence to independence to some measure of dependence again; and, second, that Mr and Mrs James and Philip all moved in step or in phase with each other. What might have happened if one of them had been out of phase with the other two? There are three principal ways in which this might occur and the consequences are different in each.

Continued dependence

If a child is born with a congenital impairment and is severely disabled, he will probably not achieve the stage of full adult independence. The parents will therefore have an adult dependent child. This involves them in a continuing, parental caring relationship with the adult child which may be a heavy physical and emotional commitment into the years when they become older, or old, and when they were expecting to resume their primarily marital relationship. It will also be appreciated that under these circumstances it is difficult for the heavily disabled, dependent adult to achieve emotional maturity and to be responsible for decisions about his or her own life. Those who do achieve maturity and responsibility may feel very frustrated by their dependency and by the assumption of helplessness that able-bodied people may make about them. Thus when one member of the family is out of phase, the feelings of being pulled two ways, of frustration and tension may be greatly heightened; and if these tensions are not resolved, a crisis develops in which a person's usual methods of coping with physical or emotional difficulties are inadequate.

The parents of a dependent, congenitally disabled child, of whatever age, usually have fears as to how he will be cared for after their deaths. The mother of a fourteen-year-old boy with cerebral palsy wrote: 'His future, when we are not here to look after him, haunts me.'[1]

Premature dependence, of slow onset

It is generally accepted that elderly people cannot always be fully independent, so that we express admiration, and some slight surprise, when an elderly person remains fully active and independent. If Mrs James had developed progressive arthritic disease in her mid-thirties and had become disabled in early middle age, she would have become prematurely dependent. In that case, she and her husband would have had early warning of possible future dependence, as the diagnosis of one of the progressive diseases carries with it the possibility of future disability. The individual and the family thus have the opportunity of experimenting with different practical methods of coping with a less active life and they have the time to make emotional adjustments, so that a family crisis may be averted.

Nevertheless, the strain on the family may be considerable. A man of fifty-seven suffered from cerebral arteriosclerosis (hardening of the arteries of the brain) which had been developing over several years. He had some loss of intellect, some paralysis and some incontinence of urine and occasionally of faeces. His wife, of the same age, said to me: 'He's like another child, not a husband, I have no freedom. I wish he would die.'[2]

Premature dependence, of sudden onset

When a person is involved in an accident or suffers some dramatic medical change in condition, impairment and disability can occur suddenly and simultaneously. Neither the individual nor the family has time to make any adjustments, and a crisis usually occurs. The person and the family may therefore need much help during the crisis period, which can usually be decreased as they begin to make their own adjustments.

A man of fifty-nine had been severely disabled by a stroke at the age of fifty-five. His wife told me: 'It has made him an old man. There is a lot of tension. My patience is running out.'[2]

One woman described her prematurely dependent husband as a child and another as an old man. Both men had become out of phase with the family life cycle: child or old man rather than middle-aged husband. Their wives were having difficulty in changing their roles in the family and their relationship with their husbands, as well as having the practical problems of caring for them.

General note

These examples demonstrate some of the practical and emotional problems which may be present in a family with a disabled member. However, not all families experience severe problems and not all experience the same difficulties; and reactions to problems are unique. The variations are manifold.

For example, a highly articulate woman of fifty-five was the wife of a sixty-four-year-old man who was severely disabled with rheumatoid arthritis. She told me:

> He's a bad-tempered man, especially since the rheumatoid arthritis got worse, but I jolly him out of it. I shelter him from family worries but we discuss a lot together—politics, religion and so on, talks on TV. His disability's made no difference as we've never had a normal life: he's been ailing for twenty-eight of our thirty-five years of marriage.[2]

People in their environments

Able-bodied people

When Mr and Mrs James had Philip, he became the centre of interest of their respective families and friendly neighbours. The Jameses brought him up according to the general practices of their families; and when Philip began to play with his cousins and, later, with the neighbours' children, they continued his informal education. In the company of other able-bodied youngsters, Philip progressed through play-group to school and, refusing to undertake higher education, started work. At each stage he influenced, and was influenced by, his contemporaries—children, teenage schoolfriends and workmates. This influence was particularly clear in his leisure pursuits and in his relations with his girlfriends.

We may think of an individual as living in the centre of a series of widening concentric circles, like the ripples from a stone thrown into a pond. As the individual grows up, so his contacts with the environment widen and ripple outwards, while the influences which these different contacts exert on the person ripple inwards, like the ripples on a pond reaching the bank and then being reflected back.

Disabled people

About the same time that Mr and Mrs James had Philip, another local couple, Mr and Mrs Andrews, also had a boy, Kevin, but he was born suffering from cerebral palsy—he was spastic. The uncertainty of most young mothers with their first baby was increased for Mrs Andrews when Kevin did not develop in the same way as Philip. He was unable to explore his body or to pull himself up to look over the side of his pram, so that his field of vision remained limited and he received less visual stimulation than Philip. Kevin could not crawl to explore his home and later was not able to play with his cousins and neighbours' children.

This was a continual physical and emotional strain for Mrs Andrews. While Mrs James could easily obtain a baby-sitter and have an evening out with her husband, Mrs Andrews's friends were afraid of the responsibility of looking after a disabled baby. At the maternity and child welfare clinic, Mrs Andrews felt depressed and was jealous of the other mothers with their healthy babies; but they did not spend much time with her, irrationally wanting to keep their babies away from a disabled baby. As this was Mrs James's reaction, Philip came to believe from an early age that disabled boys such as Kevin were 'different'.

Later, Kevin was assessed at a Family Assessment Centre and a very full picture was obtained of the family's practical and emotional difficulties and strengths. They received help and advice about caring for him at home and in due course he went to a residential school for disabled children. There he received education and care adapted to his special needs and Mrs Andrews was able to look after him during the school holidays. Thus a crisis was avoided for this family.

Another family was not so fortunate. The following is an

extract from a letter written by the mother of a five-year-old disabled girl who was being cared for by her grandmother:

> So here we are—one struggling grandmother who will have a nervous breakdown if nothing can be done soon, a worried father trying to run a business, one very puzzled three-year-old boy who cannot understand why his much loved sister does not respond to his affection and [who] wonders why she does not live at home . . . one mother who feels . . . terrified of what she might do to her daughter if she comes home again and behaves as before, and in the middle of it all, one very pretty, much loved little girl who does not understand and cannot cope with the world and whose only means of expressing herself is [by] screaming.[3]

On leaving school, Kevin lived in a hostel for young disabled people and was employed in a sheltered workshop. He therefore entered manhood after a very limited experience of life compared with Philip, and he was young for his age. He had little contact with able-bodied people outside the family circle and no girlfriends. Mrs Andrews had not had other children, in order to be able to devote herself to Kevin as the centre of the family, thus making Kevin an over-protected, rather self-centred only child. This made it difficult for him to relate well to the young people in the hostel or to be realistic about his abilities in the workshop.

Adults who become disabled later in life have major problems of adjustment, as was seen with Mr Roberts and Mr O'Reilly, but they have the advantage that their early experience was as able-bodied people. They thus have the same life-experiences as their contemporaries on which to build when they have to adjust their lives following disablement. Therefore the relationship and emotional difficulties experienced by congenitally disabled people and people with acquired disability are different in many particulars, even though there may be many practical problems in common. Both may experience lack of responsibility in the family. The wife who protected her disabled husband from family worries did so from the best of motives. (I do not think that she wanted to gain control.) But her policy excluded him from the circle of family discussion and decision-making.

Throughout their lives the James and Andrews families were subject to the influences arising from the way in which contemporary society is organized: we can think of the outermost of the concentric circles as being the organization of society, the social system, within which we live. For Philip and Kevin, the kinds of schools and opportunities for education available for their different needs were dependent on the educational system; their entry into employment and their progress were influenced by the occupational system. Provisions for the maintenance of their health and for Kevin's special needs were determined by the health and social care systems; while the social security system determined what financial assistance was available in case of sickness, disability or unemployment, and provided retirement benefits for their parents. The existence and character of these systems at any time is influenced by the economic system and by the philosophy of the political system currently prevailing.

Nevertheless, people can alter aspects of the social system. In relation to provision for disabled people, pressure is at present exerted mainly through self-help organizations and voluntary welfare organizations; but this is not sufficient. We need a growing together at the grass-roots and a mutual understanding between disabled people and able-bodied people. Then the need for pressure groups for disabled people would be diminished.

We have seen that people with physical disability are unable to perform some of the activities of daily living unless they have the help of another person or the use of mechanical aids, and this may make it difficult, if not impossible, for them to engage in some activities in society. But their range of activities may be further limited by the attitude of many, perhaps the majority, of able-bodied people who do not expect disabled people to do everything that they themselves do. Some able-bodied people experience embarrassment, as well as surprise, if a physically disabled person breaks through this invisible barrier and takes his place alongside able-bodied people.

The following published exchanges between an able-bodied man and a disabled man demonstrate many of the phenomena described in this chapter — stigma, stereotypes, prejudice —

and readers may feel that neither of the men is wholly blameless.

In 1981 an edition of *The Listener* carried a review of an autobiography by a physically disabled man who, largely through his own efforts, had gone to university, graduated, obtained two higher degrees and made his career in teaching. The review was positive but hard-hitting in places.[4] It resulted in a letter to the Editor from the author.[5] Parts of the review and of the reply are relevant to our discussion. The extracts which follow have been carefully selected so as not to distort the accuracy or the emphases of either the review or the letter:

From the review
This book delineates several diverse areas of the author's life, some interesting and attractive, others much less so. . . . At that age [eleven] he contracted poliomyelitis, which even after treatment left him paralysed in both legs, back, and right arm, and unable to walk. The onset of the illness, the subsequent therapy and surgery, his own reactions, are described with praiseworthy clarity and vividness. These pages — 20 or 30 of them — I thought the best part of the book, and it would be a shame to give away the details of their absorbing 'plot' . . .

Yes, [the author] has a heart-warming story to tell, and the will and energy he has displayed to achieve a substantial teaching career are beyond congratulation. It is a measure of his lack of self-pity, and of his overcoming of disability, that one judges much of his book *as though he were unhandicapped.* [My italics.] Though he is apt to deny it, there seems no doubt that he is an awkward cuss, more than a bit of a barrack-room lawyer, more than seldom the centre of a rumpus . . .

His claim of innocence over [a particular] fracas may be genuine, but his account of some other matters must be termed dubious — conspiracies against him at a couple of schools where he taught, for example. The facts may be correct, but he is not often completely convincing about the character of others, so that one can hardly help suspecting a touch of paranoia . . .

On the other hand, I suppose we cannot be told too often of the disabled's reaction to our usual treatment of the disabled.

From the author's letter to the Editor
Sir: I must thank [the reviewer] for his wholesome review of my book . . . But he calls me a cuss, a barrack-room lawyer and paranoid, so it must not come altogether as a surprise if I beg leave to make a couple of points.

Such cognominalization is a characteristic response in society to those who say 'No'. In labelling them sick, as troublemakers out of morbidity, the need to listen to them is dispensed with. The ultimate example of this is the Soviet treatment of 'dissidents' by putting them in institutions . . .

The problem with being so labelled is that the more you protest the more paranoid you are made to seem. But this is a risk I shall have to take. [The reviewer] says that he finds some sections of the book unconvincing and concludes therefore that I must be paranoid. These sections may not be convincing because of my inadequacies as a writer. All the incidents described in [my book] actually happened. Witnesses survive.

This was supposed to be one of the themes of the book: *disability is as much socially as physically defined.* [My italics.] In our society the disabled are often excluded from the mainstream of life not because they cannot perform social or professional roles efficiently, but because society does not wish them to.

References

1 Younghusband, E., *et al.* (eds.), *Living with Handicap.* The National Bureau for Co-operation in Child Care (1970), p. 67.
2 van Dongen-Garrad, J., Unpublished research.
3 Younghusband, E., *et al.* (eds.), op. cit., p. 31.
4 Fuller, R., Book review in *The Listener,* Vol. 105, 5 March 1981, no. 2702.
5 Giddings, R., Letter to the Editor, ibid., Vol. 105, 29 March 1981, no. 2704.

Suggestions for reading

General

Campling, J. (ed.), *Images of Ourselves.* Routledge & Kegan Paul 1981. Description by twenty-five disabled women of their lives, and their relationships with able-bodied people.
Hunt, P. (ed.), *Stigma: The Experience of Disability.* G. Chapman 1966. Autobiographical essays by disabled people. They make points which are still relevant, except the two chapters on financial provision.
Miller, E. J., and Gwynne, G. V., *A Life Apart.* Tavistock Publications 1972. A pilot study of life in residential institutions for physically disabled people and young chronic sick people.

Psychological studies of behaviour and relationships

Argyle, M., *The Psychology of Interpersonal Behaviour.* Pelican 1967. A useful book, especially chapter 7 on self-image and self-esteem.
Goffman, E., *Stigma: Notes on the Management of Spoiled Identity.* Pelican 1963. The classic work; rather too much jargon but well worth reading.
Schellenberg, J. A., *Masters of Social Psychology.* OUP 1980. An introduction to the theoretical approaches of Freud, Mead, Lewin and Skinner.

THREE

'They don't want to know'

'Well, you see, they don't want to know.' This was said to me by Mrs Green, whose middle-aged husband had recently been disabled by a stroke. The London borough in which they were living still retained a sense of identity and people had the feeling of belonging, so during the initial shock of Mr Green's illness, the family, friends and neighbours rallied round. Mr Green returned from hospital and continued the long process of medical and social rehabilitation, but as time passed the visits and offers of help became less frequent and finally stopped. Mr and Mrs Green felt deserted, almost betrayed, but they doggedly continued the slow struggle with the support of a married daughter, one faithful neighbour and their general practitioner.

Unfortunately, this desertion by friends and neighbours, and even by family, happens frequently, whether the disabled person is a child or an adult. My research[1] confirmed the widespread belief that disabled people are more isolated than able-bodied people. They are also more isolated than people who suffer from an impairment but who are not disabled by it: people like Mrs Norwich who had arthritis of the hands and feet but was independent and earned her living as a cleaner. This finding shows that it is the disability that is off-putting rather than the presence of a chronic impairment. Some physically disabled children or adults and their families may be almost ostracized — and this experience hurts.

There are two main reasons for this attitude among able-bodied people. One is that disability may make them embarrassed or uncertain how to behave and so they tend to avoid a situation which makes them feel uncomfortable. A second reason is fear. There is the fear of becoming involved, practically and emotionally, in a situation where there is no clear ending to the commitment. It has been suggested that blood donor campaigns are so successful because a donor can

40

give blood to an unknown person at stated intervals: the commitment is impersonal and strictly limited.[2] Also, the sight of the physical limitations of a disabled person may arouse the conscious fear in able-bodied people that they themselves may at some time become equally disabled.

In addition, psychoanalysts hold that people suffer from an unconscious fear of mutilation, especially of their sexual organs. Although most people are not usually aware of this fear, it may affect their feelings about disability in general, and these feelings influence the way in which they behave towards disabled people. Their reaction has some similarities to that seen in the animal kingdom when, for example, adult birds instinctively attack and destroy an injured member of their own species, or when a hen bird ejects a malformed chick from the nest. Human beings do not physically destroy their disabled members, but their unconscious fears may sometimes be destructive of a disabled person's chances of happiness as a full member of their community. This is seen in the reluctance of many people to visit or to entertain a disabled person, and in the rebuffs sometimes experienced by disabled people when they wish to join in social and recreational activities with able-bodied people. Disabled children and adolescents especially may have great difficulty in meeting able-bodied young people of their own age, and in making friendships with members of the opposite sex. In an attempt to overcome this invisible barrier, an organization has been formed in Britain with disabled and able-bodied members, which goes some way towards meeting the need for shared activities.[3]

Beside these problems of attitudes, the relative social isolation of disabled people is partly due to problems of mobility, which affect access and egress and the use of public transport. The third factor is administrative. It has been shown that the ways in which the health and welfare services are organized tend to segregate disabled people and to separate them further from social contacts with able-bodied people in the community.[4] Also, the legal requirement[5] that public buildings should have suitable access and suitable toilet facilities for disabled people is often rendered ineffective by the qualifying clause that they must be provided 'in so far as it is in the circumstances both practicable and reasonable'.

So many buildings remain inaccessible for people with severe limitations of mobility. And churches are particularly impenetrable.

It is not surprising therefore that disabled people are often isolated in their communities and that this isolation frequently includes members of their families. However, some disabled people experience feelings of loneliness even when they are not as isolated as many others. In these circumstances the disabled person may have many friendships with other people but the quality of the relationship is not satisfying.

Some disabled people living in a family consisting of two or three generations may feel very alone—family life passes them by, and the effects of the generation gap may be more marked. It has been shown too that some elderly, infirm people living with their families may receive fewer visitors than those living alone: presumably people feel that they are not as much in need.

Residents in homes for disabled people and those in homes for elderly people with some degree of disability, may also feel lonely although they are surrounded by other people. In the Netherlands, old people's homes usually consist of a series of flatlets. A single or widowed person has a bed-sitting room while a married couple have a bedroom and sitting room: each flatlet has a lavatory, a shower and a very small kitchenette. The main meal is delivered from a hot trolley, together with the ingredients for a cold supper and the following day's breakfast. People can be very isolated unless they go to the communal sitting room for morning coffee or afternoon tea, or use the hobby rooms or the occupational therapy facilities. The homes with these good facilities are often large, sometimes with as many as 300 residents.

In one such home the director and the general practitioner became very worried about the problem of loneliness. The general practitioner held a discussion on the subject with a group of the elderly residents and asked them about when they felt lonely or when they knew that others felt lonely. He received seven answers.

The first two probably apply to many people, whether they are disabled or able-bodied: when a marriage partner dies; and when the children do not visit any more. The others are directly relevant to our study of disabled people: when you are sick; when you are deaf; when you are blind; when you are becoming dependent and have to be helped; and when you are always talking to other people about your own sickness.

The director then invited the chaplains and some lay members of local churches, together with a representative of the Humanist Federation, to a meeting to discuss what contribution the churches and the humanists could make to alleviate some of the problems of loneliness experienced in homes for elderly people.

Life enrichment

Many disabled people live physically restricted lives: if their lives are further restricted by fewer social contacts, they may need some form of life enrichment.

It has been suggested that recreation, which is a process of re-creation, is usually associated with the brighter aspects of life, leaving aside the darker aspects.[6] In contrast, it is the business of rehabilitation to help people with the darker side of their life while focusing on a brighter aspect ahead.

In recreation the focus is usually on present pleasure, although some hobbies require the learning of skills which may take years to perfect. Some disabled people develop hobbies, even solitary hobbies, as a form of engagement in life and as such they are constructive. Others try to use recreation as a means to escape from the darker aspects of life: human vulnerability, suffering and mortality. However, able-bodied people do not wish to be reminded of these dark aspects either and this may be a potent reason why they are often reluctant to include disabled people in their recreational activities. This reluctance may be increased by the need for eye-level contact with people in wheelchairs or with dwarfed disabled people, which often causes embarrassment to able-bodied people.

Paul Hunt suffered from muscular dystrophy and became chair-bound at the age of thirteen. He spent most of his life in hospitals and homes for disabled people. He wrote:

For the able-bodied, normal world, we are representatives

of the things they most fear—tragedy, loss, dark and the unknown. Involuntarily we walk—or more often sit—in the valley of the shadow of death. Contact with us throws up in people's faces the fact of sickness and death in the world. No one likes to think of such things, which in themselves are an affront to all our aspirations and hopes. A deformed and paralysed body attacks everyone's sense of well-being and invincibility. . . . So they are inclined to avoid those who are sick or old, shying from the disturbing reminders of unwelcome reality.[7]

Local authorities and voluntary organizations run recreational activities for disabled people and increasingly the disabled people are taking over the running themselves. A concurrent development has been the formation of youth clubs for disabled young people and able-bodied young people in which the programme planning and execution is in the hands of the youngsters themselves. Problems of relationship can arise, however: the two groups of young people do not always have the same reasons for joining a joint club, so there is not always equality between them.

Friendships

Friendships are therefore very important. The feelings of loneliness experienced by many disabled people, whether they are isolated or not, may be due to the absence of deep personal relationships, not necessarily of a sexual nature, which Storr calls 'the relation of whole person to whole person which is the outward sign of an inward integration'.[8] It may be far more important to the disabled person or to the caring relative to have one such friendship than many superficial ones. During my research I found that when disabled people have the opportunity, they form personal friendships with able-bodied people in their neighbourhood which are as deep and satisfying to both groups as those of most able-bodied people with each other; but, for the reasons I have given, disabled people have fewer of such friendships. Perhaps people from church congregations have a special contribution to make here in the pastoral care of disabled people—remembering always that some disabled people will strongly rebuff such an offer. Paul Hunt continues: 'We are asking of people something that lies a lot deeper than almsgiving. We want an extension of the impulse that inspires this, so that it becomes a gift of self rather than the dispensing of bounty (material and other kinds) from above.' He goes on to say that 'to love and respect, treat as equals' severely disabled people who are limited physically and socially, 'requires real humility and generosity'.

Sexual relationships

But the friendships among able-bodied people are not all platonic. Young people date each other; many people have sexual experience without thought of marriage; and within marriage sexual relations are the norm—non-consummation of marriage is grounds for divorce.

What of disabled people? What do *they* say?

> One's teenage years are normally one's worst, and with me it was no exception. I think the complete realization of my hopeless situation, or so it seemed, came when I saw boys of my own age walking out with girls. Sex had suddenly assumed an importance and a new significance. The first sexual urges I experienced brought with them probably the culmination of the conflict I mentioned earlier—the conflict which sprang out of knowledge that mentally I was alert, but physically repulsive. I sat in my room alone and despaired.[9]

And another young person:

> Nobody imagines that a girl in a wheelchair is pining for love. People say that I am not unattractive and that I have an affectionate nature. I am a very emotional person and am *so keen* to be happy . . . I am longing for love. How can I keep it to myself? . . . I feel deprived both mentally and physically. I hope that what I am saying doesn't sound crude, I don't mean to be indelicate. It must be marvellous to make love with a man who cares for you. I have no idea how I can obtain information on the subject to read. We are so dependent on others, and there is no privacy for me at home. Those who are not handicapped can do things to suit themselves.[10]

The distress of people who have become disabled after living a full sexual life can be as great:

> I am anxious to put our question to you. All year I have been plagued by my inability to manage an erection any more, since a car accident turned me into an invalid. My wife and I are suffering a lot under this, and our family doctor is not a great deal of help. What do you advise?[11]

And a married woman:

> Since my back operation, we have never resumed intercourse with one another. I feel very isolated since this has been omitted. The doctor does not know what advice to give me. Our marriage will go to pieces before very long.[12]

The majority of able-bodied people who have no personal or professional experience with disabled people are shocked at the thought of sexuality among those who have physical impairments of such severity that they are disabled. During a recent conversation on this subject, a man said to me: 'How extraordinary! It never occurred to me that the disabled had sexual needs.' And a woman said: 'But I think it's a horrible idea. Sex should be beautiful.' These two comments from intelligent and usually sympathetic people typify the attitudes prevalent among the majority of the population. Disabled people are 'different from us' and do not have the same needs, and the ideal is the body beautiful as portrayed in advertisements: people who fall so far below this standard should not engage in the same sexual activities. Psycho-analysts consider that the unconscious fear of sexual mutilation is very forcefully aroused in able-bodied people by the thought of 'mutilated' people using their sexual organs, so that, in order to protect themselves from these disturbing fears, they deny the sexuality of disabled people. However, Mr A. H. Sutton, congenitally disabled by cerebral palsy and happily married to a disabled girl, writes: 'It has been my experience that sex drives are just as prevalent with the handicapped [as with able-bodied people], and sexual appetites demand some gratification.'[13]

But, again, people in general do not want to know, and it is so easy for them to betray their attitudes unintentionally.

Angie, a fourteen-year-old girl suffering from cerebral palsy, was very proficient in her school cookery class. On one occasion her teacher complimented her: 'You would have made someone a good wife.' 'What do you mean—I would have?' demanded Angie. The teacher tried to retrieve the situation: 'What I meant to say was that if you marry a disabled man, you would make him a good wife.' Today, seven years later, Angie is happily married to an able-bodied man. From her wheelchair she manages their specially adapted flat and also works as a clerical assistant in a government department.[14]

It is only in the last fifteen years or so that the sexual needs of disabled people have been openly recognized. In Britain, pioneer work was done by the Head of Personal Social Services of the Spastics Society in publicizing the needs of congenitally disabled young people, while in the Netherlands an educational psychologist and a medical specialist in rehabilitation opened up the subject in relation to adolescents and adults with congenital or acquired disability. In 1970 an international conference was held to consider the needs of disabled people and the restrictive attitudes which were prevalent in the many European countries represented. The situation was summarized in the statement: 'During an age when sexual attitudes are becoming liberalized, there is a danger that something akin to a sexual apartheid will be created for the handicapped, with one set of rules for them and another for the able-bodied.'[15]

Since then, there has been some advance in the acceptance of the sexuality of disabled people by professionals engaged in work with them but public attitudes lag far behind. This also applies to many parents of disabled young people, who tend to regard their disabled children as perpetual Peter Pans. They often need help in dealing with their children's emerging sexuality but are too embarrassed to ask for it and professionals often avoid raising the subject. In Britain, as in other European countries, there is now an organization specially concerned to give information or counselling to disabled people and their parents or partners, and guidance to professionals over problems of relationships and the sexual aspects of disability.[16]

Disabled people may experience any of the same range of

problems with personal relationships and sexual difficulties as may able-bodied people, but they may have additional problems and difficulties which are related to their disability.

Congenitally disabled children may receive even less sex education from their parents than able-bodied children, because the parents often try to deny their children's sexuality; and they may have less opportunity to learn from their able-bodied contemporaries at school or in play. Their more restricted lives may result in their entering adolescence with fewer social skills, so that they may not have the ability to make a relationship when the opportunity does arise. Lightly disabled young people tend to live in a 'twilight zone' as their self-image oscillates between that of a disabled person and that of an able-bodied person.[17] This uncertainty may increase their lack of self-confidence in relation to able-bodied contemporaries, who tend to regard them as disabled. The majority of disabled young people become sexually mature. The girls usually start to menstruate considerably earlier than able-bodied girls. If a girl has not been prepared for her first menstrual period, she may interpret the bleeding as further evidence of her physical abnormality; whereas with careful preparation she will recognize it as evidence that an important aspect of her femininity has not been affected by her disability. Disabled boys have erections and wet dreams. What do unprepared disabled youngsters make of these experiences? How do they cope?

The range of problems that may be experienced by disabled people in their sexual relationships are varied. For some disabled people, the nature of their impairment has a direct adverse effect on their sexual functioning yet leaves their sexual drives intact. A large proportion of able-bodied men and women masturbate, and disabled young people and adults are no exception. But what happens to a disabled person whose arms are paralysed or whose hands are deformed? Will others assist him or her? And should they? It is important to recognize the difference between one person helping a disabled person to masturbate as a part of their permanent sexual relationship; and a disabled person being helped by different people, almost as a technical service, when the helper is often described as a facilitator. But one must ask what is the erotogenic effect on the facilitator?

Among a second group of disabled people the sexual functioning and drives are not impaired, but indirect effects of the disability make intercourse difficult or impossible. These include pain, the partner's fear of inflicting pain, fear of the medical consequences of intercourse, and either uncontrollable body movements or paralysis. Some drugs which are prescribed for the particular impairment have side-effects reducing libido or potency. Congenitally blind people are often ignorant about the physique of the opposite sex. Blind and very deaf people may have constraints in lovemaking: the former cannot have eye-contact or are unable to pick up cues and clues from visual, non-verbal messages; while the deaf person may be unable to detect nuances of voice or small exclamations of pleasure. And 'it is extra-ordinarily difficult to make love satisfactorily if both lovers are in wheelchairs'.[18]

A third group of disabled people have no instrumental difficulties but intercourse may be adversely affected by problems of relationships. These may arise from the disabled person's self-image; or the attitude of the partner to the nature of the disabled person's impairment, or towards intercourse with a disabled person. In addition, some people, particularly wives of severely disabled men, may find difficulty in having a sexual relationship when they give their husbands much intimate nursing care.

People experienced in helping disabled men and women and their partners with their sexual difficulties emphasize the need for different levels of help. Some disabled people need factual information only, mainly of a physical or a practical nature, which they are then usually able to put into effect themselves. Others need advice as to which of several possible solutions to their problem is likely to be the most appropriate for them. The range of information and advice which may be needed is wide. An uninformed congenitally disabled young person may need basic sex education, while sexual re-education may be necessary for the adult with acquired disability. This may include information about different positions for coitus or alternative methods of lovemaking which remove the emphasis on performance and achievement of orgasm. It has been said that 'in a very real sense, sexuality may be considered as a means of the blending and submerging of two personalities into a psychological and physiological unity. In so far as sex serves this purpose, it is not essential that the feelings of bodily closeness and unity must be entirely vested in the genitalia.'[19]

Mr Bailey, a businessman in early middle age with two small children, was admitted to hospital suffering from a severe coronary thrombosis. He made steady progress, but when he was shortly due for discharge the physician advised him to refrain from intercourse for three months because of the effort involved — the equivalent of running up two flights of stairs. He was very upset as this brought home to him the seriousness of his illness, and also deprived him of the opportunity to convince himself that his sexual functioning had not been affected by his illness. After the next visiting time, his wife came spontaneously to see me. 'What has happened to my husband since yesterday?' she asked. 'He has changed: he will hardly speak to me and will not look directly at me.' When I told her of the physician's recommendation and of her husband's reaction, she was very relieved, having expected bad news about his progress. 'That's more important to him than to me,' she said. 'I can still show him that I love him and that he is still attractive.'

Many disabled people in their daily lives use simple gadgets, aids to living, which enable them to be more independent in dressing, toilet care and household tasks. Similarly, some severely disabled people and their partners benefit from using aids to loving, which can be obtained from reputable manufacturers and are becoming more widely accepted by disabled people with certain impairments.

Some disabled people and their partners need counselling instead of, or in addition to, information and advice. Counselling is a process whereby people are helped to identify the details of their problems and then encouraged to make their own decisions about ways of resolving or ameliorating the difficulties. This method of help is particularly necessary when a person's emotional reaction to his or her sexual difficulty is the main trouble or when it complicates a basically physical problem. Anyone who wishes to give sexual counselling to a disabled person or the partner must first come to terms with his or her own sexual feelings; and must be at ease with disabled people and accepting of their sexuality. Involuntary non-verbal signs which betray a counsellor's negative attitudes can complicate the disabled person's problems.

Finally, it is necessary to remember another group of physically disabled people—those who are homosexual in their relationships. They are a minority within a minority and their problems of social handicap are therefore very great. Their personal suffering may be acute, as their opportunities for finding a sexual partner are even more restricted than those of heterosexual disabled people. Organizations now exist to help them with their particular difficulties.[20]

This chapter has examined a range of personal relationships from childhood friendships, through neighbourly companionship, to mature sexual relationships; and the sexuality of disabled people has been considered in this wide context. In all these relationships disabled people may be at a disadvantage, partly by reason of their disability itself but also because of the attitude of many able-bodied people who 'don't want to know'.

References

In preparing this chapter, I have been indebted for helpful discussion to Dr Mary Davies, Education and Training Officer, Association for the Sexual and Personal Relationships of the Disabled, London, and Dr A. Verkuyl, formerly Director of De Hoogstraat Rehabilitation Centre, Leersum, The Netherlands.

1 van Dongen-Garrad, J., Unpublished research data from community health surveys.
2 Titmuss, R. M., *The Gift Relationship.* Allen & Unwin 1970.
3 Physically Handicapped and Able-bodied (known as PHAB). The address is 42 Devonshire Street, London W1.
4 Sainsbury, S., *Registered as Disabled.* Bell 1970.
5 Chronically Sick and Disabled Persons Act 1970. Ch. 44, section 4, para. 1.
6 van Dongen, J. C., *Recreatie.* Orgaan van de Stichting Recreatie, July 1968, no. 3.
7 Hunt, P., 'A critical condition', in Hunt, P. (ed.), *Stigma: The Experience of Disability* (G. Chapman 1966), pp. 155, 156, 158.
8 Storr, A., *The Integrity of the Personality* (Penguin, 1972), p. 175.

 9 Sutton, A. H., 'Marriage and the handicapped', in Lancaster-Gaye, D. (ed.), *Personal Relationships, the Handicapped and the Commuunity* (Routledge & Kegan Paul, 1972), p. 110.
10 Heslinga, K., Schellen, A. M. C. M. and Verkuyl, A. *Not Made of Stone.* Leyden, Stafleu's Scientific Publishing Co., 1974. English translation. Quotation, p. 11.
11 ibid., p. 11.
12 ibid., p. 11.
13 Sutton, A. H. op. cit., p. 111.
14 Campling, J. (ed.), *Images of Ourselves.* Routledge & Kegan Paul 1981. Quoted in *Community Care* (October 1981), p. 14.
15 Loring, J. A., in Lancaster-Gaye, D. (ed.), op. cit., p. 83.
16 Association for the Sexual and Personal Relationships of the Disabled (SPOD), 14 Peto Place, London NW1 4DT.
17 Dechesne, B. H. H., *Lichamelijk Gehandicapte Jongeren: Sexualiteit, Relaties, Selfbeeld.* Rotterdam, Lemniscaat, 1979. (Physically handicapped youngsters; sexuality, relationships, self-image. Research by a priest who is also a philosopher and psychologist.)
18 Loring, J. A., op. cit., p. 85.
19 Hohmann, G. W., quoted by Verkuyl, A., in Vinken, P. J., and Bryun, G. W. (eds.), *Handbook of Clinical Neurology,* Vol. 26, part ii, p. 455.
20 Information about organizations for homosexual men or women may be obtained from the Association for the Sexual and Personal Relationships of the Disabled (SPOD), 14 Peto Place, London NW1 4DT.

Suggestions for reading

Greengross, W., *Entitled to Love: the Sexual and Emotional Needs of the Handicapped.* National Marriage Guidance Council in association with the National Fund for Research into Crippling Diseases 1976.

Greengross, W., *Sex and the Handicapped Child.* National Marriage Guidance Council 1980.

Relationships and the Physically Disabled: an Introduction for Counsellors. A booklet produced by the Association for the Sexual and Personal Relationships of the Disabled. Nine SPOD advisory leaflets on separate topics are also available.

Stewart, W. F. R., *The Sexual Side of Handicap: a Guide for the Caring Professions.* Woodhead-Faulkner 1979.

Toward Intimacy: Family Planning and Sexuality Concerns of Physically Disabled Women. Human Sciences Press 1978.

FOUR

'It's how I *feel* that matters'

I first heard about Richard Salisbury when he was twenty-three and doing his teachers' training course. From being a highly motivated pupil at grammar school, where he had done very well in A-levels, he had gone on to university and obtained a good degree in mathematics. He had successfully completed the first part of his theoretical studies in a post-graduate teachers' training course and was in the middle of his first period of teaching practice. To the surprise of his practical work tutor, he was having more than the usual difficulties of students at this stage.

The tutor and I discussed the young man's background in relation to his present difficulties. His father was a successful headmaster, popular with his staff, the pupils and their parents. He was also a good teacher who continued to do some teaching in his subject of physics, while his all-round prowess as a sportsman gained the added respect of the boys. Richard secretly adored and admired his father, and his determination to emulate him as far as possible was the motivation for his hard study at school and university and for his choice of career. Unhappily, Richard was congenitally disabled, suffering from a locomotor impairment which resulted in paralysis of the legs and great weakness of the arms. He could operate with one hand an electric wheelchair and typewriter but was in other ways very dependent physically. He hated his body and interpreted his parents' balanced, helpful attitude as being motivated by pity, so his attitude towards his father was often ambivalent. As his self-image fell so far short of his ideal, he tried to compensate by being fiercely competitive in his studies, and his inner hostility towards his 'competitors' frequently showed in his verbal aggression. This was particularly apparent when he was forced to ask for physical help, which he felt was humiliating.

During his teaching practice, Richard used his typewriter

and an overhead projector instead of the traditional blackboard. He did not prepare his lessons well, as he considered
them to be of such a simple standard. As he had attended a
residential grammar school for disabled boys, he did not
realize that not all boys are as motivated to learn as he had
been: he failed to apply his theoretical knowledge of methods
of teaching and he could not hold the boys' interest. In
addition, he did not make any reference to his disability or to
his unusual method of displaying his teaching material; as a
result, the boys' curiosity about their disabled teacher was an
added distraction for them. Richard recognized that the
classes were not successful, but he blamed this on his
disability which prevented him from standing up to see what
the boys at the back were doing. He became anxious when
his achievement was so much less than he had hoped, and
when this failure was repeated he became depressed.

When it was his turn to lead a discussion group with his
fellow students, he did most of the talking and made no
attempt to draw the others into a discussion. Why should he?
To him they were his competitors. The students recognized
his failure but told him that he had done 'all right': they felt
that they could not be honest with a disabled man and tell
him how bad he was. (Such over-protection occurs frequently
and is not helpful, as the disabled person is denied the social
feedback that is given to others to enable them to make a
realistic assessment of their achievements and abilities.)
Consequently, Richard thought that he was a great success
as a group leader; he had held the floor and he found that
very satisfying.

Here was a young man whose motivation was not the
enlisting of young people in the adventure of learning but a
self-centred, driving ambition to achieve the same success as
his idol. His pupils were not people in their own right but the
means whereby he would obtain his goal. His fellow students
were not men and women with whom he shared a common
enterprise, but his competitors. He could not countenance
failure as due to lack of ability on his part, so he blamed it on
his disability.

Richard had problems arising from his motivation; from
his personal relationships; from the difference between his

self-image and his ideal self-image, related to his belief that disability was a stigma; and from the difference between his attainments and his aspirations. It was no wonder that he felt hostile, was verbally aggressive and became anxious and depressed.

As I listened to Richard's tutor describing the young man's perplexing behaviour as he and the students saw it from the outside, I realized again how impossible it is to help people with their difficulties until one knows how they themselves see the problems and, even more important, how they feel about them. As the tutor and I talked and more information emerged, it became possible for me to describe Richard's behaviour in relation to his feelings, in the same way that I have written about them here. The tutor then saw what his own task was and in what ways he could try to help Richard.

Richard's experience raises the question as to whether other disabled people have similar feelings of hostility and aggression, of anxiety and depression, and whether their feelings are equally intense. It also raises the question as to what proportion of all physically disabled people feel this way. These were the questions to which I tried to find answers in one stage of my community health surveys.

The answers may be obtained from two complementary sources. The medical profession and associated professional staff accumulate a wide experience of the feelings of disabled people when they are treating newly disabled patients or caring for those who have been disabled for a longer time. But most disabled people are in hospital for relatively short periods and many are not cared for by professionals. Therefore the experience of professional people may be selective and it may not relate to disabled people in general. However, their detailed experience can be put into perspective by health-survey information about people living in the community.[1] It is then possible to compare the feelings of disabled people with those of their able-bodied neighbours and of those people who suffer from an impairment but are not disabled by it.

In everyday life most people feel aggressive or anxious or depressed at times, but the feelings are transient and not severe. But if the feelings are severe and persist, as with

Richard, the person has become emotionally disturbed. This introduces the two concepts of mental health and emotional disturbance.

Mental health

Mental health is even more difficult to define than general health, but a widely accepted definition describes six characteristics of mentally healthy people.[2] They can acknowledge their own feelings and they have a strong sense of personal identity, of being 'me': as did Mr O'Reilly (ch. 2). They have a sense of direction, can provide their own driving power, and can take an independent line of action: Mr Roberts (ch. 2) did not have these characteristics.

They are resilient to emotional stress and are not overwhelmed by their own emotions or by feelings of guilt: Mr O'Reilly again. They are realistic, seeing things as they are rather than as they would like them to be, and they can appreciate the feelings of others: Mr O'Reilly and Mary Hamilton (ch. 1) showed these characteristics while Mr Roberts did not. Their emotional responses to new situations are appropriate: like Mr O'Reilly's and Mary Hamilton's and unlike Mr Roberts's.

These six characteristics are usually in a state of balance in each individual. There are differences between people, and some individuals show certain characteristics more clearly than do others but the differences between people in good mental health are not extreme.

Newly disabled people who are distressed are showing an appropriate response to a crisis; and mental health includes the ability to be appropriately disturbed. But if such emotional disturbance continues for years after a crisis, it ceases to be appropriate; the person ceases to be in good mental health and has become emotionally disturbed. I have not used the term mentally ill because this is not what I mean. In our physical health, we sometimes feel off-colour without being really ill; but it is an unpleasant state to be in and if it lasts for a long time it can badly affect our family life and our work. So we do what we can to pick up again as quickly as possible. This is the nearest analogy that I can offer to being emotionally disturbed.

Emotional disturbance

In my community health surveys, I compared the proportion of physically disabled adults who showed signs of emotional disturbance with the proportion of able-bodied adults of the same ages in the same community who showed signs of emotional disturbance. I also compared these two groups with people who suffered the same range of impairments but who were not disabled. These comparisons enabled me to see whether the development of emotional disturbance is related to suffering a chronic impairment, or whether it is related to the state of being disabled. I shall give here a summary of my findings in general terms.[3]

I first compared able-bodied adults and people of the same ages who suffered an impairment but who were not disabled: I found that the proportion of people who were emotionally disturbed was approximately the same in both groups. I concluded that the development of emotional disturbance is not related to suffering an impairment. The comparisons I now make are between disabled people and able-bodied people.

Physically disabled adults

Among disabled men, up to a half show signs of emotional disturbance compared with one-twentieth of able-bodied men. Emotional disturbance occurs ten times more frequently among disabled than among able-bodied men.

Among disabled women, the proportion showing signs of emotional disturbance is about a half, i.e. the same as among disabled men. Less than a quarter of able-bodied women show signs of emotional disturbance. Emotional disturbance occurs more than twice as frequently among disabled as among able-bodied women.

Disabled men and women, more than their able-bodied contemporaries, show evidence of depression and hostility and of the phenomenon of repression — forcing feelings 'underground'. These emotional reactions are more severe among disabled than among able-bodied people. Depression is the most marked reaction. We can generalize and say that the proportion of disabled people who are depressed is greater than that of depressed able-bodied people, and that they tend to be more depressed.

In general, the emotional disturbance develops after the onset of disability and it is a reaction to the state of being disabled and not to the impairment causing the disability. It occurs more frequently, and in a more severe form, among disabled adults whose mobility is very limited, than among disabled people whose disability affects mainly other activities of daily living. It occurs more often among the younger disabled adults than among the older disabled people; and it is particularly marked among the younger disabled men. To summarize, the people in a community who are at the greatest risk of developing emotional disturbance are the younger disabled men whose mobility is severely restricted.

All these differences are statistically significant, which means that they could not be due to chance: they are genuine differences between disabled adults and able-bodied ones.

Physically disabled children

My researches were carried out among adults and exactly comparable information about children is not available. However, it is known that among able-bodied children aged ten or eleven, about one child in twenty suffers emotional disturbance.[4] (This is the same proportion that I found among able-bodied men.) Emotional disturbance may be observed among children suffering from impairments of a non-neuro-logical kind such as diabetes, asthma, heart disease and malformations of the skeleton. The proportion is about one in every seven disabled or impaired children.[5] This is more than twice as many as among able-bodied children.

The possibility is strong that physically disabled children, as well as adults, are at greater risk of developing emotional disturbance than their able-bodied contemporaries.

Families with a physically disabled member

We know very little as to how the experience of living with a physically disabled member of the family affects the mental health of other family members in the long term. More information is available about the effects of living with a member of the family who is mentally ill or mentally retarded. However, physical disability, mental illness and mental subnormality have two characteristics in common: they can disrupt the lives of the sufferers and of members of their families; and, unhappily, they are still often regarded as a stigma. Studies relating to mental illness and mental retardation, together with what little information is available in relation to physical disability, may give us some clues as to how physical disability may affect the mental health of the relatives of a physically disabled person.

The research findings reveal that the mothers of physically disabled children or mentally retarded children are at greater risk of developing minor illnesses, with 'nervous symptoms', than the mothers of able-bodied children from the same community.[6] The children,[7] adult relatives[8] and marriage partners[9] of mentally ill people are at risk of developing emotional disturbance or physical illness with 'nervous symptoms'. The cumulative stresses may lead to a breakdown in marriage more frequently than among married people as a whole.[10]

It was with this background knowledge that I extended my studies with physically disabled people. I found that the proportion of physically disabled married women who are divorced or separated is greater than among able-bodied married women from the same community. There is no difference in the proportion of married disabled and married able-bodied men who are divorced or separated. Perhaps we may conclude that men are less tolerant of a disabled wife than wives are of their disabled husbands.

I compared the mental health of the wives of a group of disabled men and the mental health of the wives of men who suffered from the same impairments but who were not disabled. I found that a larger proportion of the wives of the disabled men suffered from emotional disturbance than the wives of the non-disabled men with the same impairments.

It is safe to conclude that experience of physical disability exposes the sufferer to an increased risk of developing emotional disturbance. There is sufficient evidence to alert helpers to the probability that family members are also at greater risk.

Material and practical problems

I have dealt in detail with the emotional responses to physical disability because pastors are most likely to be involved with this aspect in their caring work with disabled people and their families. However, physical disability usually results in material and practical problems of various kinds and different degrees of severity. Sometimes these problems are so pressing that disabled people and their families cannot benefit from help with their emotional problems until their practical difficulties have been alleviated.

I summarize these practical difficulties in Chapter 9, but one aspect must be stressed here. Many of the different practical difficulties experienced by disabled people have one aspect in common—they are caused or increased by the person's lack of mobility. Emotional disturbance occurs more frequently, and more severely, among disabled people whose mobility is very limited. Therefore any aspect of the person's physical or social environment which further limits his or her mobility may be an important factor in the development of emotional disturbance.

References

1 Community Health Surveys: In a community health survey, it is usual for a carefully selected proportion of the community to be examined. The people are selected for inclusion in the study in such a way that they are representative of all the people in the community. The findings of the study can then be applied to the community as a whole. Some members of the public are cynical about such surveys because similar methods are used by organizations which conduct opinion polls, and these are sometimes held in disrepute. This is unfortunate, as scrupulous attention to method can produce reliable information.

In health surveys of the kind which I conducted, information is usually obtained by means of a carefully constructed interview or a well-designed questionnaire. Reliability is increased by giving the research assistants a careful training. The advantage of this method is that the people in the community are able to speak for themselves and the influence of the research worker on what they say is reduced to a minimum.

2 Jahoda, M., *Modern Concepts of Positive Mental Health.* New York, Basic Books, 1958.

3 Garrad, J., 'A controlled epidemiological study of psychological disturbance among disabled adults living in the community', in *British Journal of Preventive and Social Medicine.* Vol. 29 (1975), p. 61.
'Impairment and disability: their measurement, prevalence and psychological cost', in Lees, D., and Shaw, S. (eds.), *Impairment, Disability and Handicap.* Heinemann 1974.
van Dongen-Garrad, J., Additional unpublished data.
4 Rutter, M., and Graham, P., 'Psychiatric disorder in 10- and 11-year-old children', in *Proceedings of the Royal Society of Medicine.* Vol. 59 (1966), pp. 382-7.
5 Rutter, M., 'Psychiatric aspects of multiple handicap: some epidemiological findings'. Paper read to the International Study Group on Neuropsychiatry. Alfriston 1967.
6 Rutter, M., Tizard, J., and Whitmore, K. (eds.), *Education, Health and Behaviour* (Longman 1970, ch.21.)
7 Rutter, M., *Children of Sick Parents.* OUP 1966.
8 Sainsbury, P., and Grad, J., *The Burden on the Community.* OUP 1962.
Grad, J., and Sainsbury, P., 'Problems of caring for the mentally ill at home', in *Proceedings of the Royal Society of Medicine.* Vol. 59 (1966), p. 20.
Sainsbury, P., and Grad, J., 'The cost of community care and the burden on the family', in Lees, D., and Shaw, S. (eds.), op. cit.
9 Nielson, J., 'Mental disorders in married couples', in *British Journal of Psychiatry.* Vol. 110 (1964), pp. 683-7.
10 Brown, G. W., 'Measuring the impact of mental illness on the family', in *Proceedings of the Royal Society of Medicine.* Vol. 59 (1966), p. 18.

Suggestions for reading

The development of the personality and how emotional disturbance and mental illness can arise:

Erikson, E. H., *Childhood and Society.* Pelican 1965. A difficult book, but chapter 7, 'The Eight Ages of Man', is worth the effort.
Lowe, G. R., *The Growth of Personality: From Infancy to Old Age.* Pelican 1972. Excellent. Lucid. Based on Erikson's theories.
Storr, A., *The Integrity of the Personality.* Pelican 1972. Excellent. Clear and sympathetic.

Physical disability

Wright, B., *Physical Disability—a Psychological Approach.* Harper & Row, N.Y. 1960. The classic work. Clear, non-technical, with many case histories and a good index.

Emotional disturbance and mental illness

Brown, G. W., and Harris, T., *Social Origins of Depression.* Tavistock Publications 1978. The results of a study carried out among women.
Hooper, D., and Roberts, J., *Disordered Lives — An Interpersonal Account.* Longmans 1967.
Rycroft, C., *Anxiety and Neurosis.* Pelican 1970.

FIVE

The whole person

It is often said that man is body, mind and spirit. In the Bible we are told: 'Thou shalt love the Lord thy God with all thy heart, and with all thy soul, and with all thy mind, and with all thy strength' (AV).[1] Without getting involved in this chapter in a discussion of dualism or in a metaphysical analysis, we can say that these are different aspects of a man, a woman or a child in all his or her totality: aspects of the whole person. Therefore people react as whole individuals, not just by one aspect of themselves: and they react to a situation as a whole, even though one aspect of the situation may temporarily affect their reaction more than other aspects. In this chapter I use this approach to study the situation of a disabled person in a community.

Disability as crisis

Mr O'Reilly (ch. 2) was admitted to hospital after the initial shock of becoming disabled had passed. He was experiencing feelings of anxiety, depression, humiliation and anger which were complicated by his initially poor relations with the medical and other staff. When he had accepted my offer of help, I gave him the opportunity to put all his feelings into perspective, and I helped him to do so. Then he began to see that these emotional responses were not entirely justified and were unhelpful to him, and that the future was not completely hopeless. He gradually adopted a more positive, constructive attitude towards finding new ways of co-operating in his treatment. He and his wife started seeking new, positive aspects in their relationship which had been severely changed by his impotence.

However, situations that are experienced as crises for one person may not affect another in the same way, because

individuals value the different people, objects and circumstances in their lives according to their own scale of values.
Similarly, people react to crises in their own way which is
characteristic of their own personality, their usual behaviour
and their attitude to life in general. But certain similarities
can be seen in everyone's response to a situation which for
them is a crisis.

Disability, of sudden onset

When this crisis occurs, people initially experience a state of
shock. There is a period of numbness, of disbelief: 'I can't
take it in', 'I can't believe it'. As the numbness wears off and
they begin to realize the significance of their changed
condition, they become anxious. This anxiety is followed by,
or accompanied by, depression as they realize more fully the
details of their new situation. During this second phase they
feel, and usually are, unable to cope emotionally with the
situation or with their feelings. Their anxiety causes them to
worry, but worrying is a form of work which can be very
constructive. In the whole person there are no short cuts:
anxiety has to be lived through and worked through, and it is
usually liberating to be able to express it. This may mean that
people have to get worse emotionally before they can get
better. This can be a distressing phase and the sufferer may
be frightened by the strength of his or her emotions. The
helper must be readily available to listen and to absorb some
of the emotion. Depression is associated with grief for the
loss of the former self: the body-image has changed and with
it the old self-image, and the person does not yet know what
his or her new self-image is or will be.

Mrs Rosalind Chalmers was disabled by poliomyelitis at
the age of twenty-seven. She has written:

> I have said that no one, after emerging from a serious and
> cataclysmic illness, is the same person again. He might
> think he was or would be, but for good or evil he would be
> different. The components are still there, naturally, but
> reassembled, some diminished and some enlarged, until
> the result is a variation on the theme of his old self, which
> until he is familiar with the score he has to play by ear. At

the same time he has the same family and commitments as before. They do not change.[2]

Grieving for the loss of the old self is also a form of emotional work and the loss has to be grieved through in the same way that anxiety has to be worried through. When this worry work and grief work have helped to alleviate the anxiety and depression, sufferers enter the third phase, in which they try to find their new self-image, their new identity and new ways of coping with a totally new situation. Because their former practical and emotional ways of coping with life may no longer be possible or adequate, they must develop variations on these old ways or find new ones. This is often a process of trial and error. Help offered at this point may help them to minimize the error.

As men or women begin to make these emotional adjustments and to adapt their usual way of living to meet the changed situation, they start to regain some of their lost self-confidence; and they feel able and are able to cope with their altered lives with the same emotional competence as before. (This experience is represented by line A of Figure 1 on page 66.)

When people develop positive responses after a crisis, they are usually enabled to continue their good personal relationships with the people in their lives. Sometimes their response to the crisis may lead to an enrichment in their relationships with other people, particularly if they are close. Sometimes a man and wife will say that the experience has drawn them closer together. One woman developed a progressive impairment when in her early thirties, from which she was to die young. She told me that her relations with her husband were much deeper 'because now, neither of us takes the other for granted'. For some people, the experience of a crisis can be a period of personal and emotional growth, so that their eventual ability to cope with the stresses of life is increased. Part of this growth may be due to the feeling of having survived a very testing experience: a feeling of 'if I can get through that, then I can get through anything'. If people cope well with one crisis, then the chances are that they will cope well or even better with another, because they will enter it with some measure of confidence knowing that they survived the previous one. It is an example of the old adage, 'Nothing succeeds like success.' (This experience is represented by line B of Figure 1 below.)

But some people do not regain the same emotional ability to cope with life as they had before the crisis. Mr Roberts (ch. 2) is an example of this response. He showed signs of intellectual denial and emotional withdrawal, which were his continuing reaction to having become disabled. During the year prior to his admission to hospital, he had not been able by trial and error to make any emotional adjustment to his developing disability; and he had not received any offer of help with this emotional difficulty. So he did not regain his former level of emotional functioning. (Line C of Figure 1 below.) Thus when he experienced the second crisis of being cured of his disability, he was less well equipped emotionally to deal with it, and was less able to use the help I offered him. His final level of emotional functioning could therefore be represented as lower than line C in Figure 1.

People who do not regain their former emotional ability to cope with life are usually those who cannot face the significance of the crisis, and so they block off. They deny

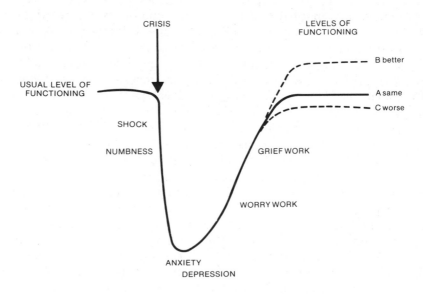

Figure 1   Emotional reactions to a crisis

intellectually the significance and the long-term consequences of the crisis. They do not do their worry work or their grief work, and so they get stuck in the second phase and their anxiety and depression do not lift. The anxiety and depression may continue as obvious symptoms or they may go below the surface: in either case they reduce the person's ability to cope with daily life and they have an adverse effect on personal relationships.

Disability, of slow onset

If a crisis is foreseen, most people become anxious in advance. With some people excessive anxiety can be paralysing while others become over-active in unproductive ways; but a level of anxiety which people can tolerate usually makes them do something about the cause of the anxiety. If they cannot avert the coming crisis, their anticipatory anxiety results in their doing some of their worry work in advance, so that when the crisis hits them, their reactions of shock, anxiety and depression are usually not so severe and their emotional recovery is usually somewhat quicker.

For example, in a study of men and women who had to undergo a major operation, it was found that one group showed much anxiety before the operation and just as much afterwards: they were the chronic worriers who worried about everything in life. A second group showed some anxiety, which seemed a realistic response under the circumstances. They were able to discuss their anxiety and they responded well to reassurance. After the operation, they showed only a little anxiety and they coped well with the post-operative treatment. These people had started their worry work before the operation. A third group showed no anxiety before the operation; they blocked off, they denied the seriousness of their situation. After the operation, they showed great anxiety and much hostility, and found it very difficult to tolerate the post-operative treatment.[3]

When a person is suffering from a slowly progressive impairment, the resulting disability is of slow onset and can be envisaged as a series of downward steps. The person therefore has the opportunity to do some worry work and grief work for each of the stages of the illness. This was the

reaction of Mrs James. The experience of people with a
progressive disabling impairment resembles in some ways
that of people who have recurring periods of non-disabling
illness throughout their lives: the next bout of illness is not an
unexpected shock; many of the characteristics of the illness
are known to them and they know what to do about them;
there may be one or two new features but these are relatively
small and the experience of the previous bout of illness can be
used in learning how to cope with them. Therefore many
disabled people may understand their disability and know
how to cope with it better than a doctor who sees them
infrequently. The stress comes when a particular milestone is
reached. With Mary Hamilton (ch. 1), the milestone was
reached when her slowly deteriorating eyesight became so
poor that she could not continue in her usual employment
and had to train for different work.

Congenital disability

Here the situation is very different because the disabled
person has no experience of being able-bodied. Initially, the
baby or young child does not realize that he or she is any
different from anyone else. As self-awareness increases and
their knowledge of other people widens, they begin to notice
that they cannot do things that other children do and that
they have to undergo treatment that others do not; and they
may observe that their bodies are different in some ways
from others'. This awareness of disability is therefore
incremental. Each stage in a disabled boy's or girl's widening
contacts with their families and the community demonstrates
to them the extent of their own 'differentness'. In this way,
their feeling of being set apart may start early in life. The
child and the adolescent therefore experience their disability
as a series of crises, a series of losses, as they progressively
realize what they have never had. They usually react with
grief, and perhaps anger, at each realization. It is only when
they are old enough to understand the nature of the
impairment, and what their condition as adults is likely to be,
that they can do any anticipatory grieving.

The period of adolescence is a difficult time for able-bodied
youngsters as they search for a new self-image, a new identity,

in passing from childhood to adulthood, and as they experience their newly developing sexual needs. This phase is made more difficult for congenitally disabled adolescents because they may not have a complete self-image and their body-image may not be acceptable to them — as we saw with Richard Salisbury (ch. 4). Thus they may not have a clearly appreciated or acceptable identity when they enter the transition phase during which their bodies and their emotions change with the physical and emotional maturation of approaching adulthood.

These experiences may be contributory causes for the relative emotional immaturity which may be observed among some congenitally disabled young people. As a result, they may be less well equipped to deal with the pressures of adult life than able-bodied young people. The pressures on disabled people are greater anyway, and these are not always reduced when parents try to protect children and adolescents from them.

Disability, as bereavement

Bereavement is a special and very acute form of crisis. Murray Parkes made a study of men and women who had had a leg or an arm amputated.[4] He demonstrated that they show many of the same emotional responses which he frequently observed among men and women who had been bereaved by the death of their marriage partners. There is the process of realizing the loss; a period of alarm with feelings of anxiety, tension and restlessness. The subsequent 'searching' process does not occur in the same way but the men and women tend to show the same preoccupation with their loss. Then 'he mourns for his lost intactness, particularly at times when this is forced on his attention' and 'each frustration brought back a period of painful pining for the world that was no longer theirs'. The fourth feature is shown when the newly disabled people have feelings of bitterness, or of envy of able-bodied people. Intense anger may be directed against the surgeons or others involved in the amputation. Like the widow or widower, disabled people often blame themselves for their loss. The fifth feature, feelings of internal loss of self or of mutilation, is common. Murray Parkes quotes two men: 'You sometimes feel you've had part of your body taken away and you're no longer part of the world — they've taken part of your life away'; and 'You feel mutilated, you know you'll never be the same again . . . *Underneath* I feel badly damaged.' Murray Parkes comments that 'underneath' reflects the injury to the self whose intactness has been shattered. This is related to the severe changes in the person's self-image and body-image.

People who have lost a loved one sometimes identify with that person; people who have lost a limb do not show this identification phenomenon, unless the experience of the phantom limb may be so described. This is the phenomenon when amputees feel that the amputated limb is still in place and they frequently experience pain in it. Murray Parkes thinks that this phantom-limb pain may be a way of expressing difficulty in accepting the loss of the limb. He says that, as in abnormal reactions of bereavement following the loss of a loved person, there is sometimes 'a distortion or a prolongation of the process of realizing the loss and . . . it does appear that one of the main types of reaction found among disturbed widows and widowers is also found among amputees — chronic grief'.

The first five of these reactions were seen in the example of Mr Roberts (ch. 2) during his period of disability. They were more clearly in evidence with Mr O'Reilly (ch. 2), as he was able to express his feelings openly and he knew that he would have considerable permanent disability.

Mr Williams (Introduction) was an example of chronic grief. As his chronic bronchitis progressed, his increasing breathlessness forced him into increasing inactivity. He was not a reading man. Previously he had studied the sports pages of the newspapers, but these now reminded him of his early manhood when he had been athletic, and he could no longer bear to think about those days other than to regret their passing. He had previously enjoyed strip cartoons in illustrated papers but now he had no appetite for sexy pictures. He considered occupational therapy or craftwork to be only for women. So he just sat, breathless and brooding.

Murray Parkes concludes his description of newly disabled people by saying:

It does seem that the psychological transition from being

an intact person to being an amputee is a painful and time-consuming process which is, in many ways, similar to the transition from married person to widow or widower. It would seem justifiable, therefore, to regard these two situations as part of the same field of study and to consider what can be learnt from one that would be of value in preventing or treating the pathological [abnormal] forms of the other.

If we compare loss of able-bodiedness as a result of a limb amputation with loss of able-bodiedness through other impairments, we see that they each have several characteristics in common: there is the loss of intactness and/or loss of function with associated changes in the body-image and self-image; there are changes in the ability to perform some of the activities of daily living, and changes in relationships with able-bodied people. The experience of professional people in the medical setting supports the view that very many disabled people may experience bereavement in a similar way to those people disabled by amputation.

Bowlby, writing the foreword to Murray Parkes's book, describes bereavement as 'a major hazard to mental health'. I think we are justified in regarding chronic grief, or other manifestations of abnormal grieving following the loss of able-bodiedness, as being one of the explanations why a larger proportion of physically disabled people show signs of emotional disturbance than do able-bodied people.

Aspects of the whole person

Some people regain their usual level of emotional functioning after disability and their mental health is not adversely affected. Others do not recover in this way but show continuing signs of emotional disturbance. What happens during the period of depression and anxiety or during the later phase when these symptoms usually begin to lift, which influences some people in the direction of emotional recovery and good mental health? Or which influences others in the direction of emotional disturbance? What happens at the cross-roads? If we knew this, we might be able to stand at the cross-roads ready to help disabled people take the route towards mental health rather than that leading to emotional disturbance. If we missed them at the cross-roads, we might be able to catch them up before they were too far along the road to emotional disturbance and help them retrace their steps towards mental health.

We can gain some understanding of these phenomena by considering the aspects of the whole person. I think there are four aspects to the whole person: biological, psychological (of which the emotional component is important in this context), environmental and behavioural. These aspects are continually interacting to maintain a state of equilibrium. As our first example of this interaction we examine Mary Hamilton's experience (ch. 1). We remember that as her diabetes progressed, her eyesight became worse (biological aspect). With her poor eyesight she could no longer do her work properly (behavioural aspect). Her poor performance (behavioural) caused her much anxiety (emotional) and this had an adverse effect on her diabetic balance (biological). There was thus a circular effect: biological—behavioural—emotional—biological. (This is represented in Figure 2a on page 74.)

The physician and I tried to break this vicious circle. We suggested that Mary should make a change in her environment by going to the assessment centre for assessment of her work potential. The encouraging report made at the centre (environmental) improved her morale (emotional) and this was reinforced by her unexpectedly good relationships with her fellows (emotional). These constructive experiences counteracted her anxiety (emotional) so that its adverse effect on her diabetes (biological) was reduced and her diabetes again became stabilized (biological). So here the sequence was environmental—emotional—biological. (See Figure 2b on page 74.)

In the first stage, the adverse effect of Mary's anxiety was cancelling the good effects of her medical treatment. In the second stage, changes in her environment resulted in hope for the future which overcame her anxiety about it. When her anxiety was counteracted, her medical treatment was again effective. It may be helpful to think in terms of physical interacting forces: if a tug is pushing a barge (the modern method), it is exerting a force and the barge moves forward. If a second tug is attached at the front and pulls while the first one pushes, two forces are exerted which augment each other. If, however, the two tugs are pulling in opposite directions, the barge will move in the direction of the tug which exerts the greatest force, as in a tug of war between two teams. In my conception of the whole person, there are four forces which continually interact. (The complete interaction of the four aspects of the whole person is represented in Figure 2c on page 74.)

When something occurs which influences one aspect of a person, there are repercussions in the other three aspects of the whole person; and this applies to adverse influences and to positive influences. When offering help or care to disabled people and their families, it is useful to make an analysis of the situation in this way; and to discuss with them which aspect should be influenced first in order to produce the greatest beneficial effect. Sometimes a person has an emotional problem with which the pastor can give considerable help: but at the same time the practical problems in this person's environment are so big that they must be tackled first, because anxiety about them prevents any improvement in the emotional difficulties. With Mary Hamilton (ch. 1), her environment was changed from one which caused anxiety to one where her positive experiences effected a lessening in her anxiety over her future employment prospects. It then became possible to help her with her continuing fears of becoming totally blind.

There is therefore another dimension to be taken into account—that of time. As these four aspects or forces are interacting over time, help given at any point in time may have an immediate effect, which is very satisfying to the helper. Or the disabled person may benefit much later, perhaps after contact with the helper has ended, and this deprives the helper of the satisfaction and reassurance of knowing that he or she is effective.

For the second example showing the interaction of the different aspects of the whole person, I have chosen the experience of bereavement, because we have seen how important this may be in the life of a disabled person. The effects of bereavement have been summarized by Murray Parkes.[5] During bereavement, men and women tend to consult their general practitioners more frequently than before with

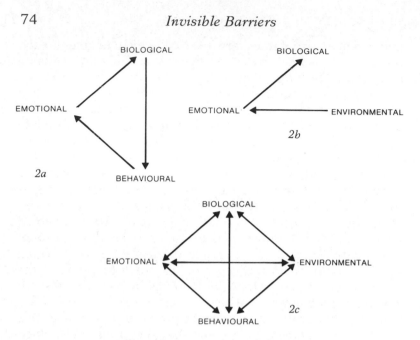

Figure 2 Aspects of the whole person

some physical illness which requires treatment: and some
may use this illness as an excuse to ask the doctor for help
with personal problems that have little to do with their
physical condition. Widows and widowers have a higher
mortality rate than married men and women of the same age;
so do bachelors and single women; but the striking feature
of the increased mortality among widowed people is that
most of the deaths are found to occur during the first six
months of bereavement. For example, among a group of
widowers over the age of fifty-four, the death rate was seen to
increase by 40 per cent during the first six months and then
to decrease to that of married men of the same age. The
largest proportion of these extra deaths were due to different
forms of heart disease. (Murray Parkes makes a reassuring
comment in parentheses: 'In case any bereaved reader is now
clutching his chest and preparing to call an ambulance, may I
hasten to point out that palpitations and a feeling of fullness
in the chest are normal concomitants of anxiety and that
bereaved people often experience them without developing
heart disease.')

The conclusions which Murray Parkes draws emphasize the interdependence of the four aspects of the whole person. He says:

> I think we can justly claim that many widows and widowers seek help during the months following the death of their spouse, and that the professional persons they most often go to are medical practitioners and ministers of religion. I accept the evidence that bereavement can affect physical health and that complaints of somatic anxiety symptoms, headaches, digestive upsets, and rheumatism are likely, particularly in widows and widowers of middle age. Finally, there are certain potentially fatal conditions, such as coronary thrombosis, blood cancers, and cancer of the neck of the womb, which seem in some cases to be precipitated or aggravated by major losses.

Conclusions

If we think of the onset of disability as a crisis and in particular as a crisis of bereavement, we see that the equilibrium of the four aspects of the whole person may be severely upset; and that this state of dis-equilibrium may be followed by a new state of equilibrium which involves physical illness or emotional disturbance. Help offered at the time of crisis should therefore have the aim of assisting the disabled person to achieve a new state of equilibrium which avoids these adverse consequences. By taking account of all four aspects of the whole person, and by bringing about a change in whichever aspect it will be most effective, it is possible to help men and women achieve a new and satisfying equilibrium which enables them to retain their mental health.

I should like to repeat something that I said earlier and which has been implicit throughout this chapter. By the term whole person I am referring to the person in his or her totality. A person who has lost a limb or whose body is incomplete in some other way, or who is mentally retarded or has become senile, is just as much a whole person as the person whose body is complete or who is mentally able. I am using psychological and religious language. Psychoanalysts tell us that no one is ever completely whole psychologically,

76 *Invisible Barriers*

as we all have our areas of difficulty. Theologians tell us that we are not whole, there being only one perfect Man. Nevertheless, the concept of wholeness is the goal towards which members of the caring professions strive, for themselves and for those whom they are helping.

Bill Kyle has written:

If we are to understand man—in his totality and complexity—we need to understand the insights that have come to us from science, behavioural studies, and so on. By a thorough understanding of the needs of the human personality, we can more effectively deploy the ministry so that the Church touches man at points of deep need. If we can bring together the insights of religion and an understanding of how the human personality functions, the resulting synthesis will be good and strong, and will help us to encourage personality growth.[6]

References

1 Mark 12.30.
2 Chalmers, R., in Hunt, P. (ed.), *Stigma: The Experience of Disability* (G. Chapman 1966), p. 27.
3 Janis, I., quoted in Caplan, G., *An Approach to Community Mental Health* (Tavistock Publications 1961), p. 51.
4 Murray Parkes, C., *Bereavement. Studies of Grief in Adult Life* (Tavistock Publications 1972), ch. 11.
5 op. cit., ch. 2.
6 Kyle, W., *The Wholeness of Man*. The Westminster Pastoral Foundation Booklet 1980.

Suggestions for reading

Crisis

Caplan, G., *An Approach to Community Mental Health.* Tavistock Publications 1961.

Bereavement

Marris, P., *Loss and Change.* Routledge & Kegan Paul 1974. The author develops the thesis that in each crucial transition 'the anxieties of change centre upon the struggle to defend or recover a meaningful pattern of relationships'.

Murray Parkes, C., *Bereavement. Studies of Grief in Adult Life.* Tavistock Publications 1972.

Speck, P. W., *Loss and Grief in Medicine.* Baillière Tindall 1978.

The whole person

Balint, M., *The Doctor, the Patient and the Illness.* Pitman 1968.

CIBA Foundation, *Physiology, Emotion and Psychosomatic Illness.* Amsterdam, 1972. (In English).

Dodge, D. L., and Martin, W. T., *Social Stress and Chronic Illness.* University of Notre Dame Press, 1970.

Dubos, R., *Man, Medicine and Environment.* Pall Mall Press 1968.

SIX

'I have no choices'

None of us knows precisely what lies ahead of us; but for some disabled people the future may be even more uncertain, while others may feel, with some despair, that it holds 'just more of the same'.

Dependence

Our study of physical disability so far has shown that disabled people may be physically dependent on other people in ways which range from minimal assistance to total care. Those people who need help with toilet and menstrual care, or with feeding, usually find the necessity for such intimate care very difficult to accept because of its association with babyhood; while the help which some disabled people require in meeting their sexual needs may diminish their feelings of masculinity or femininity.

A disabled woman may need help with the care of her children and in running the home. When Mrs Rosalind Chalmers was disabled by poliomyelitis at the age of twenty-seven, she had a little girl of two years and a baby boy of a few weeks. After two years in hospital, she came home to find that the girl had forgotten her. The boy had never known her. She had a series of resident housekeepers for about ten years and was then admitted to a Cheshire home for disabled people. Writing about the ten years at home, she says:

> In my husband's case he had lost his wife, but she was not conveniently dead and buried. ('Daddy had three children,' said our daughter pertinently, 'me, Peter and Mummy.') . . .
> As for the children, they had lost their mother. Instead of being desired for themselves, they were someone's job of work which had to be attended to. Oddly enough it is the small things I remember most clearly and painfully. . . .

When I heard one or other of them cry in the night I would try to judge the urgency of the cry to decide whether I should wake the housekeeper, who would not be pleased, and thus not likely to be very patient with them. But they didn't cry much; perhaps not as much as they ought to have done. . . . No one was actually cruel to the children; some people were very kind. But one continuing, reassuring presence was lacking, and when they were hurt I couldn't put my arms round them.'[1]

The usual policy in the rehabilitation of disabled people is to help them become as independent as possible. But how independent is 'as possible'? A policy which is now followed increasingly, especially with spastic and spina bifida children, is to work towards planned dependence.[2] Instead of patient, staff and relatives striving to achieve a level of independence approaching 'normality', a target is mutually agreed which is realistic and achievable. This avoids the disappointment of failure and enables the person and family to know in advance what kind of help, and how much, he or she will continue to need. Once the target has been reached the person may, if it is possible, aim for another target of greater independence: but this is an extra, and no one is under pressure. This step-by-step increase in independence gives encouragement and a sense of achievement.

Not all disabled people can accept this policy of planning to accept a level of independence below 'normality', as they find it too threatening. Yet none of us is fully independent of others, physically or emotionally. Psychiatrists speak of mature dependence, by which they mean that a person is only complete when he has satisfying personal relationships and he has accepted the basic need of human beings for each other. Mature dependence is 'a relationship involving evenly matched giving and taking between two differentiated individuals who are mutually dependent, and between whom there is no disparity of dependence'.[3] This description refers to the mutual emotional dependence between two people. However, where this exists, it is possible for the disabled person to recognize that while he or she is additionally dependent in a physical way on the other, the other is dependent on him or her in some other way. So again we recognize the importance of reciprocity.

Miss Audrey Shepherd, a teacher and Methodist preacher, disabled in her late twenties, discusses this aspect:

> Independence is generally thought of as being of great importance, but how important *is* it? Are any of us independent, anyway? Are we not, rather, interdependent? Of course, it is worth trying, if it is at all possible, to be independent in the everyday things of life — washing, dressing, getting around the house, etc. When the disability in question is the paralysis following polio, often the years bring increasing independence, as one is able to work out new ways of doing things. But I think that too much emphasis on independence can breed fanaticism. If I am in the wheelchair at school, it bothers me not at all if somebody pushes it along for a bit, making a joke of having something to lean on. Why not? Yet I have known those who go tense with rage and are quite rude if any help is offered.
>
> This seems to me to be getting things out of proportion. The able-bodied are helped by their friends and help them in all sorts of ways. Why do we want to put ourselves outside this mutual help by which society exists, and insist on self-help?[4]

Disabled people react differently to the problem of physical dependence; but one reason why some, perhaps the majority, of people resent it is due to the feelings of obligation and of a difference in status that arise from being always on the receiving end.

Receiving

We read in the New Testament that it is more blessed to give than to receive;[5] but Blau has argued that in a situation of 'social exchange' the person who gives has more power and prestige than the person who receives. When one person gives a service to another, the giver places the recipient under an obligation, which the recipient can only discharge by providing some service to the first person in return.[6] To test the accuracy of this statement, we have only to think of the people who say: 'I do not accept hospitality because I cannot afford to return it.' In addition, it is services or actions which are performed voluntarily which tend to engender most feelings of personal obligation or gratitude. If goods or services are paid for, one feels that one has a right to them, and feelings of gratitude are not normally aroused in the recipient towards the supplier. But if there is an imbalance of obligation, the recipient not only has less status than the person supplying the services but also has less power. Mrs Rosalind Chalmers has written:

> In theory I was in charge of the house. I didn't need much actual nursing and was in a wheelchair all day, but I needed someone to get me up, put me to bed and take me to the lavatory. It is extraordinarily difficult to reprimand anyone when they lift you on and off the lavatory like a baby several times a day! In addition, I had to think of the repercussions on the children. . . . So I interfered as seldom as possible in the running of the house, and if that too was humiliating for me I considered my humiliation to be the lesser evil.[7]

A person who is dependent on the services of another may, if he or she is able to do so, take one of four courses of action to avoid being placed in the power of the giver. These are, first, to provide services which are needed by the giver in exchange, i.e. reciprocal service; second, to obtain the services from an alternative source as well, in order to avoid renewed obligations to the one giver; third, to secure the service by force; fourth, to go without the service. But Mrs Chalmers was not able to give her housekeeper any reciprocal service; it was hard enough to find one housekeeper, let alone two at the same time; she could not use force; and she could not go without the services. So she remained in the power of the housekeeper and tolerated the humiliation for the sake of her children.

A simpler and more common experience is that of people who need the services of a home help from their local authority. They are required to have their incomes assessed to determine how much they must pay for the service. People who object must either pay the full amount or go without the service.

Pinker analysed the national health service and the national insurance and assistance provisions.[8] He studied them as systems of social exchange, as described above, to determine whether their characteristics increase the status of the recipients or result in stigma. He shows that most people make a sharp distinction between those who give one of the services and those who receive it. He shows that self-help and independence are very highly valued in our society: we expect people to stand on their own feet; we admire and approve of people who struggle to do so in the face of great difficulties; we are apt to despise people who, in our opinion, give up too easily. Therefore we tend critically to observe the users of the health and social services, especially those who draw monetary benefits, to see whether they are genuinely in need, whether they are really dependent on the service or benefit. Pinker argues that every dependent group in our society is a threat to the autonomy of the self-supporting. This can be clearly seen in the different attitudes held towards people who draw contributory benefits as of right, such as sickness or unemployment benefits for which they have contributed in times of employment so that there is reciprocity; contrasted with attitudes held towards people who draw non-contributory benefits, for example those who receive only supplementary benefit where there is no reciprocity. Sometimes one hears such people being referred to as scroungers receiving money which they have not earned.

Disabled people use the health and social services more frequently than able-bodied people and a larger proportion receive all their income from sickness or unemployment benefits, supplementary and other non-contributory benefits. One would expect this to be so, and it has been demonstrated in many studies including mine. Disabled people, therefore, are more likely to be placed in a dependent position as recipients than able-bodied people are, with the associated feeling of being powerless and stigmatized. Pinker concludes his analysis by saying: 'If the dominant human impulses were compassionate, we would expect that the greatest of human tragedies such as irretrievable loss, chronic dependency, the process of dying and death itself, would attract a prior claim on welfare resources. This is clearly not the case.'[9]

Paul Hunt has examined the difficulties created for disabled people by their frequent inability to reciprocate and by the consequent stigma of dependency:

> We are often useless, unable to contribute to the economic
> good of the community. As such . . . we cannot help posing
> questions about values, what a person is, what he is for.
> . . . Most people regard anything not visibly productive as
> expendable. Contemplation, philosophy, wisdom, the
> liberal arts, get short shrift from the average man. Those
> who cannot work, such as the sick, the aged, the
> unemployed, are subject to a tremendous pressure to feel
> useless, or at least of less value than the breadwinner. . . .
> Obviously we who are disabled are deeply affected by the
> assumptions of our uselessness that surround us. But it is
> vital that we should not accept this devaluation of ourselves,
> yearning only to be able to earn our livings and thus prove
> our worth. We do not have to prove anything. . . . Our
> freedom from the competitive trappings that accompany
> work in our society may give us the opportunity to
> demonstrate its essential elements. Also we can act as a
> symbol for the pre-eminent claims of non-utilitarian
> values . . .
>
> At the ultimate point we may only be able to suffer, to be
> passive through complete inability. Just here we have a
> special insight to offer, because our position gives us an
> extra experience of life in the passive aspect that is one half
> of the human reality. Those who lead active lives are
> perhaps especially inclined to ignore man's need to accept
> passivity in relation to so many forces beyond his control.
> They may need reminding sometimes of our finiteness, our
> feminine side in the hands of fate or providence. We are
> well placed to do this job at least.[10]

I think we are justified in concluding that dependence may
cause emotional and attitudinal difficulties for many disabled
people, and that it may be a contributory cause of the
emotional disturbance experienced by a large proportion of
them.

Giving

Men and women seem to have a biological and psychological
need to give, to help. In Britain, blood donors give their blood

voluntarily and free of charge: in the USA, blood donors receive cash payments. A comparative survey of blood transfusion services was made by Titmuss to provide the material for a study of the gift-relationship, a study of altruism in modern western society.[11] He writes: 'Man is not born to give'. The new baby is self-centred and demanding, but by the time he is adult he has learned to give and to give 'to unnamed strangers irrespective of race, religion or colour—not in circumstances of shared misery but in societies continually multiplying new desires . . . concerned with property, status and power.' In western societies there is a strong urge in many people to give. This activity is approved in our culture and, especially in Christian communities, unselfishness and altruism are highly valued attributes.

But if receiving can cause problems for recipients, does not-giving cause problems for would-be givers? Titmuss says that to deny men or women the opportunities of expressing their need to give, is to deny them the opportunities to enter into gift-relationships with other people. He argues that gift-relationships in modern society 'signify the notion of fellowship'—*les petits cadeaux entretiennent l'amitié*; and fellowship can be thought of 'as a matter of right relationships' which have a basis in the structure and function of society.

Titmuss claims that ethical considerations and the aims of social policy both focus on 'integrative systems . . . which promote an individual's sense of identity, participation and community; and allow him more freedom of choice for the expression of altruism and which, simultaneously, discourage a sense of individual alienation'. If giving promotes a person's sense of identity, participation and community, and discourages a sense of individual isolation, then giving would seem to be even more important for the disabled person than for the able-bodied person. So we return again to the concept of reciprocity.

Reciprocity

We have seen that one of the ways in which a recipient can avoid being stigmatized or placed in the power of the giver is by becoming a giver also. A simple example is provided by the following anecdote. A parish in Britain started a Good

Neighbour Scheme: members of the congregation visited other members, or non-members living in the parish, who were thought by the minister or by others to be in some kind of difficulty. A middle-aged teacher, Miss Elliott, who had recently joined the congregation, was asked by the minister to make regular visits to a retired nurse, Miss Bradford, who had long been a member but who was now, through ill-health, often confined to her flat. He briefly discussed this proposal with both women, separately, in advance. When Miss Elliott made her first visit, Miss Bradford welcomed her and provided tea and biscuits, a token of welcome and of reciprocity. After several visits, Miss Bradford told Miss Elliott that the minister had asked her to agree to the visits as a way of helping a newcomer to settle down in the congregation. Miss Elliott was very taken aback, as she did not consider that she was in any kind of need, and felt that she was quite capable of settling down through her own efforts. It was only when she discussed this with a friend that she realized that Miss Bradford, a member of a caring profession, clearly felt that she did not need any help either. Each expected to give without being in need of receiving.

Miss Elliott felt that the minister had been less than honest with them both and that he had been very manipulative. She told him so. If he had been frank with both women, they might have been able to discuss with him and with each other their mutual giving and receiving; and the visits might have led to a rewarding reciprocal relationship. As it was, there was unspoken resentment on both sides and the visits soon petered out.

It is therefore very important that helpers should be fully aware of this problem, and that they should discuss with disabled people both sides of the giving and receiving relationship and the disabled people's reciprocal giving. Paul Hunt has pointed out that disabled people can contribute by 'being' and by challenging popular value systems. While some disabled people may recognize this as an important contribution, others may feel the need for a more obvious method of reciprocation; so givers should study with the disabled person how he or she can also give. Audrey Shepherd has written about this question of values and reciprocation:

It can never be a question of going back to the old life in spite of what has happened, but of going forward into a new life because of what has happened. Now the disabled person offers himself to the community in a different way, because he has new limitations but also because he has new insights. The community is helped to remain whole, for the strength and tenderness of the able-bodied are needed. The disabled one is also helped. He is lifted from self-centredness into the life of the community as a whole.[12]

When a disabled person is always dependent on others, whether this dependence is physical, financial or emotional, he or she experiences feelings of obligation and stigma; feelings of being in the power of another, of being dominated.

A dominating future

De Juvenel contrasts the concept of a dominating future with the concept of a masterable future.[13] He argues that for every person the future is divided into these two parts. The masterable future is that part which people can alter, which they can influence, which they can control. The dominating future is that part over which they have no control, the part in relation to which they are powerless. De Juvenel continues with the observation that, in human affairs, the future which is dominating as far as the individual is concerned may be masterable by someone else, a more powerful person, acting on his or her behalf.

While the dichotomy of a dominating or masterable future applies to everyone, I think that disabled people have control over a smaller part of their present lives and their future than able-bodied people, because fewer alternatives are open to them. Disabled people are more dominated.

To take a few obvious examples: many disabled people are more restricted than most able-bodied people as to the kinds of work they can undertake and how far, and by what means, they can travel to work. As a result, during a time of recession and increased unemployment, they are at a greater disadvantage in obtaining alternative work and are more likely to experience prolonged unemployment. In the spring of 1981,

15 per cent of the registered disabled people capable of work were unemployed, compared with the national figure of 10 per cent; the average period of unemployment for disabled workers was nine months compared with less than four months for able-bodied people.[14] Disabled people are more controlled by impersonal economic forces.

Disabled women may have to rely on other women to run their homes for them and to accept the helpers' methods and standards, as Rosalind Chalmers described. Entry and exit to their homes and all kinds of buildings are controlled by the structure of the building in relation to the nature of the individual's impairments and the severity of the disability. This limitation further controls opportunities for work and many aspects of daily activities.

The nature of their impairment and the severity of their disability control the part that some disabled people are able to play in family life. I quoted the remark made to me by one wife that she sheltered her husband from family worries. Although she did this from the best of motives, she excluded him from the circle of family discussions. In some families there has to be reversal of the usual roles, when a wife works to support her disabled husband; or when a husband runs the home for his disabled wife as well as working to support the family. When there is a disabled child in the family, it has been shown that the mother tends to remain at home with him while the father takes the other children for the usual family outings. So the control can extend to members of the family also.

A crucial aspect of the dominating future for many disabled people is the progressive nature of their impairments with the near-certainty of increasing disability and dependence. For example, many neurological impairments are progressive; and I showed in the Appendix to Chapter 1 that progressive chronic bronchitis and other chronic lung diseases and arthritic diseases are the two impairments which result in the largest numbers of disabled people. Finally, my research showed that the death rate among disabled adults is five times that of the men and women of the same ages in the same community. For secular man, death is the ultimate domination.

In our culture, where a high value is placed on

independence, the difficulties involved in the giving and receiving of help of all kinds are central to the social and psychological problems associated with disability. Increasing dependence among people in the older age groups is more acceptable to members of the community and to many of the older people themselves; but this toleration is not always extended to people in the younger age groups, who usually find dependence extremely hard. This may partly account for the fact that a larger proportion of younger disabled people, especially men, show signs of emotional disturbance than do the older age groups. The extent of a disabled person's dependence on others is only partly within his or her control, being mainly determined by the nature of the impairment and the severity of the disability in relation to the social environment. The person's dependency relationship in the community is also part of the dominating component of life.

A Quaker has said that, if men and women are to achieve their full potential and to be fulfilled, they need to be able consciously to choose their own way and to enter into life and activities of their own free will.[15] But a disabled person usually has fewer opportunities to do this than an able-bodied person. Paul Hunt referred to 'so many forces outside [man's] control':[16] and another disabled man recorded disabled people's 'rebellion against the fate which prevents us from doing such minor chores for ourselves'. He continued: 'It is not so much the big services which injure our pride as the necessity of asking for a multiplicity of small ones.'[17] This limitation of choice and of independent action are particularly frustrating for those disabled people who by temperament are independent and self-motivated.

It does seem that disabled people, more than their able-bodied contemporaries, are dominated and are aware that they are dominated by a variety of forces over which they have little or no control. A young, newly-qualified graduate, who had become confined to a wheelchair by a progressive locomotor impairment, was having a talk with me about his employment prospects. After an open and frank conversation, it was possible for me to ask him what was the worst part of being disabled. After a thoughtful pause he replied: 'Not being able to do as I want. I have no choices.'

Hope

Many disabled people experience more uncertainty about the future than most able-bodied people and a greater part of their lives and their future is outside their own control: while others feel that their lives are without purpose. It may be that one of their greatest needs is for hope. By this I do not mean optimism, which, by comparison with hope, is a shallower and less realistic attitude.

Macquarrie calls hope a universal phenomenon.[18] He says that in many of the activities of our lives

> there is an affirmation of the future, a trust in the future, an investment in the future. It seems that in almost everything we do, we are projecting ourselves ahead of ourselves, and we are doing it in the expectation or at least in the faith that some goal will be achieved. If . . . 'hope is only faith in relation to the future', then virtually everything we do is done hopefully.

He argues that hope has emotional, volitional and cognitive aspects—it involves our emotions, our actions and our thinking—and in developing this argument he makes a number of statements which are relevant to our consideration of the needs of disabled people and their families. He shows that hope is vulnerable and may easily turn to fear; and how the disappointed person 'quite literally wilts'; and he quotes Proverbs 13.12: 'Hope deferred makes the heart sick.' Perhaps disabled people are more vulnerable than others in this respect also.

When discussing the relation of hope to freedom, Macquarrie says:

> Hope implies that there is, so to speak, an empty space before us that affords us room for action; or to put it in a slightly different way, an open road along which we can choose to move. Where everything is foreclosed, there is no hope. Thus hope is inseparable from human freedom and human transcendence. This in turn means that hope belongs essentially to any truly personal existence. Where freedom is denied, whether in practical terms through

oppression, or in theoretical terms through some deterministic ideology, hope is denied also; and where hope is denied, persons are being destroyed, for to be a person means, among other things, to be constantly projecting oneself in hope towards goals in which personal being will find fuller expression and satisfaction. So we can say that where there is hope, there is freedom, and where there is freedom, there is hope.

The relation of this argument to de Juvenel's concepts of the masterable or dominating future is obvious.

Macquarrie quotes St Thomas Aquinas: 'Hope's object is a good that lies in the future and that is difficult but possible to attain.' He continues by discussing a person's response in the face of intractable circumstances and points out that 'true hope lives in the awareness of the world's evils, sufferings and lacks'. He accepts that inaction and resignation may sometimes be necessary but argues that

> this would not be the inaction of despair or the dissolution of hope into despair. . . . There are circumstances in which resignation does not necessarily mean the abandonment of a fundamental hopefulness. Resignation may not be passive surrender; it may be an active acceptance of the intractable circumstances of the situation, followed by a new attempt to face and deal with the situation including these threatening circumstances.

He recalls the prayer associated with Reinhold Niebuhr: 'God, give us grace to accept with serenity the things that cannot be changed, courage to change the things that should be changed, and the wisdom to distinguish the one from the other.' He discusses the word serenity which, he says, 'is equanimity, an affirmative composed accepting frame of mind, and one that testifies to the inward strength of the serene person . . . Thus, although hope normally spurs and sustains action, it knows also how to be quiet and patient.'

Hope involves a philosophy of life. 'It carries in itself a definite way of understanding both ourselves and the environing process within which human life has its setting. Particular beliefs about ourselves and the world underlie and express themselves in all experiences of hope.' Macquarrie analyses these beliefs and shows that they involve seeing the world 'as a project of man's existence and transcendence'; and speaks of hope having a creative function, 'as co-operating in the shaping of an unfinished world'.

Has the Christian offering help to a disabled person and his family a particular contribution here, too?

References

1 Chalmers, R., 'Victim Invicta', in Hunt, P. (ed.), *Stigma: The Experience of Disability* (G. Chapman 1966), p. 22.
2 Gardner, L., 'Planning for planned dependence', in *Special Education.* Vol. 58 (March 1969), no. 1.
3 Storr, A., *The Integrity of the Personality* (Penguin 1972), p. 42.
4 Shepherd, A., 'One body', in Hunt, P. (ed.), op. cit., p. 61.
5 Acts 20.35.
6 Blau, P. M., *Exchange and Power in Social Life.* John Wiley 1964. Ch. 4, 'Social Exchange' and ch. 5, 'Differentiation of Power'.
7 Chalmers, R., op. cit., p. 23.
8 Pinker, R., *Social Theory and Social Policy.* Heinemann Educational 1971. Ch. 4, 'Exchange and Stigma'.
9 ibid., p. 172.
10 Hunt, P., 'A critical condition', in Hunt, P. (ed.), op. cit., pp. 149-50.
11 Titmuss, R. M., *The Gift Relationship.* Allen & Unwin 1970. Especially ch. 13, 'Who is my stranger?'.
12 Shepherd, A., op. cit., p. 65.
13 de Juvenel, B., *The Art of Conjecture* (Weidenfeld 1967), p. 52.
14 *Spastics News.* May 1981. Quoting Manpower Services Commission.
15 Aarek, W., *From Loneliness to Fellowship.* Allen & Unwin 1954.
16 Hunt, P., in Hunt, P. (ed.), op. cit., pp. 149-50.
17 Ford, R., 'Quite intelligent', in Hunt, P., op. cit., p. 42.
18 Macquarrie, J., *Christian Hope* (Mowbray 1978), pp. 4-15.

Suggestions for reading

Blau, P. M.; Macquarrie, J.; Pinker, R.; Titmuss, R. M.: as above.

SEVEN

'Where is God in all this?'

Clergy and lay people offering pastoral care or counselling to physically disabled people and their families may be asked a number of ethical and religious questions. These fall into three broad groups. The first two groups involve dilemmas of choice: problems related to sexuality, marriage and child-bearing; and issues of life and death. Although these are primarily ethical questions, there is a large religious component, for some people who are not committed Christians too. The third group are questions related to the problem of suffering. As such they involve people's religion or their philosophy and world-view.

Some of the questions raised are the same as those asked by able-bodied people, particularly in relation to suffering of any kind; but most of the questions arise precisely because the questioner is disabled or is the relative of a disabled person. Therefore the principal difference in such counselling, compared with counselling able-bodied people, is that it is essential for counsellors to have some knowledge of the disability involved and some understanding of its effects on the life of the sufferers and their families. Only thus can the counselling be relevant.

In this chapter I focus on the questions as they relate to disabled people and their families, while in Chapter 10 I discuss them in relation to the giving of help.

Ethical questions

Sexuality, marriage and childbearing

Sexuality. I have already discussed this topic in some detail but it is worthwhile to repeat a few points in this context. The parents of congenitally disabled children are often disturbed by their children's emerging sexuality and by the question whether masturbation is wrong. The majority of able-bodied people find the thought of sexuality among disabled people very disturbing; while the need of some severely disabled people for the use of mechanical aids or the help of a facilitator raises ethical questions for some of them and for able-bodied people.

One of the unhappy aspects is the aura of voyeurism that may surround sexuality as a result of the intrusive attitudes of some able-bodied people. Angie, aged twenty-one, recorded a conversation with the gas man:

> As he was leaving the flat he turned and asked if I was married. I told him I was. Then a funny look came into his eyes and he asked if I had sex. I was shocked at his question, and at first was stuck for words. Then I was angry and said the first thing that came into my head — 'Yes, do you?' He looked embarrassed and hurried away. Since then I have been asked that question several times in different ways, most often by men.[1]

Marriage. Many disabled people have made very successful marriages with able-bodied people and, especially in the case of deaf or blind people, with partners suffering the same disability. In the last fifteen years or so, there has been an increase in the numbers of severely disabled people who have married a partner who is equally disabled. This increase seems to be due to several interacting developments. The gradual change in attitude of parents and the public towards the sexuality of disabled people, and to the possibility of successful marriages, has reduced opposition; and concurrently there has been some increase in the opportunities for disabled people to have wider social contacts and to make friendships and relationships with people of the opposite sex. These slow changes make possible a greater maturity and freedom of choice among disabled people. In addition there has been an improvement in the housing facilities, with greater variation in the accommodation, and in the community services for disabled people.[2]

In 1969 an international conference was held of '62 Clubs' which are social clubs run for and by disabled people. There it was suggested that opportunities should be provided for couples planning or contemplating marriage to meet and discuss their problems together and with social-work staff who understood their special needs and difficulties. Since then the Spastics Society in Britain has held short residential courses for engaged couples, and one of the social workers who attends is a marriage guidance counsellor.

The topics for discussion which the disabled people find the most relevant and interesting include sexual relationships; parenthood; advice on mutual self-help and independence. Other problems which the couples anticipate, and about which they sometimes ask for information, relate to finance, housing, residential accommodation and domestic work.

As this trend in marriage has continued and, increasingly, severely disabled people are contemplating marriage and a full life in the community, helpers may be asked for advice on any of these topics. They may be asked the same questions by people planning to live together without marrying.

Childbearing. This is one of the major issues for a disabled person contemplating marriage or a permanent relationship. There are the obvious problems of how a disabled person, particularly a disabled woman, can care for a baby and growing child, but with careful forethought and planning these difficulties can usually be overcome.

A less obvious but ethical question which couples sometimes worry about is whether it is fair to a child that he should be born, by intent, to a disabled parent, when it is known that this may cause emotional problems for the child. Additionally a boy may have difficulty in developing a masculine self-image if his father is disabled, while a girl may have problems of femininity if her mother is disabled. These reactions are not inevitable, but they are one of the risks, and at adolescence they may be exacerbated. One congenitally disabled man has recorded how his teenage son did not wish his school friends to see him with his father, and he did not bring them home. Also, the child may be required to do extra household tasks and perhaps help in caring for the disabled parent, at an early age, and may therefore miss out in some of his or her childhood. Rosalind Chalmers wrote:

It is a mistake to imagine that in such circumstances, and

having to do so many things for themselves, children will grow up more independent than others. On the contrary, they will grow up less so. Having no basic security, they lack confidence and grow timid and withdrawn, clinging to what there is to cling to. It is the secure child who leaves his home and possessions confidently, knowing that they will be there when he returns.[3]

A third problem is that of the possibility of a child inheriting a disabling impairment. There are a number of impairments which are hereditary and others in which the tendency to develop the disease is hereditary. When this possibility is known or thought to exist, genetic counselling may be obtained at a number of hospitals. The couple therefore can obtain information on which to base their decision.

A fourth set of questions relates to contraception and termination of pregnancy. If a couple decide to get married but not to have children, contraceptive advice is necessary; and when the woman is disabled, the method of contraception employed is of great importance. The question may arise as to whether an unplanned pregnancy should be terminated if there is a risk that it may damage the health of the disabled woman, or if the couple doubt whether they could or should bring up a baby. It also arises if there is the possibility that the baby may have a congenital disabling impairment. Medical and genetic advice is available and an investigation can be made of the foetus in the womb to determine whether the baby suffers from one of a number of congenital disabling impairments. It is only possible to test for the presence of certain congenital impairments, not the whole range.

Issues of life and death

On 15 November 1981, the leading article in the *Guardian Weekly* began:

Dr [—], the Derby paediatrician, has been found not guilty of attempting to murder a Mongol baby who died three days after birth last year. A week earlier, two men were found guilty of aiding and abetting suicides and one of them was sent to prison for two and a half years. Between these two cases extends a continuum of human suffering which most of us prefer never to think about and which only forces itself upon our attention as a result of cases like these. Between them also stretches a tangled skein of unresolved dilemmas, philosophical inconsistencies, and contradictions. The issues they have raised are among the most profound we can discuss; beyond legal precedents, beyond medical ethics, they form the moral basis of how we live.[4]

When I wrote about these issues fifteen years ago,[5] the problems which were then exercising the minds and emotions of professional staff and the general public arose over the new heart transplant operations and the use of new machinery which enabled a 'person's' circulation and breathing to continue even when his brain was dead. But the issues are still the same. Must attempts be made to keep a person alive under all circumstances and at all costs? Is it ever right to allow a person to die when he is dying? Is it ever right to initiate dying—that is, is it ever right to kill another or to co-operate in another's suicide? And is it ever right to commit suicide? These are the distressing issues with which relatives of disabled babies and adults, and disabled people themselves, are sometimes faced, and with which they may need help.

The survival of a severely disabled baby. The parents of any baby who is disabled at birth usually have ambivalent feelings about him: feelings of protectiveness for such a helpless and disabled infant; shock at the sight of his disability; feelings of guilt that, as they are responsible for his conception and birth, so in some vague way they must also be responsible for his disability; feelings of rejection; feelings that it is all too awful to face.

These ambivalent feelings complicate the distressingly difficult decisions which parents may be called upon to make in conjunction with a paediatrician and surgeon: decisions which must be made at a time when the mother is only just delivered of the baby, when her hormone balance has changed and may be contributing to emotional swings. At this point, the parents' need for counselling by someone outside the immediate medical environment may be very great, to complement the information and counselling available from the medical profession.

As an example, think of a baby who has been born with severe spina bifida. An immediate operation on the severely malformed baby may enable him or her to survive the next few weeks. If the infant survives, the parents and surgeon usually feel committed to a long series of operations, sometimes extending through the teenage years, in an attempt to reduce the disability of the child who has been kept alive. I have known parents who have agreed to the initial surgery and others who have not. One couple had a little girl who was very severely disabled by spina bifida. They refused surgery and took her home and cared for her devotedly, supported by their family doctor and the social worker, until she died a natural death at the age of three. They considered that they had acted in her best interests and their consciences were clear. After her death, they felt able to have a second child.

Ending life. The three questions I posed at the beginning of this section relate to three different policies of caring for people of any age who suffer a severe and perhaps progressive impairment, or for people of any age who are dying, even if their dying extends over a long period. There are the policies of care which aim to prolong life; those that hasten death; and those that make possible a natural death.

Some professional staff and members of the public feel that life is so sacred that a baby, child or adult must be kept alive at whatever cost to the person and the relatives. Other people think that with dying people of any age it is justifiable, and humane, to allow them to die. This may be done by not using life-saving measures such as surgery, blood transfusions or antibiotics, among other treatments. Or it may be done more positively by using certain drugs to relieve the person's pain which have the additional effect of shortening life. Some people think that doctors should be authorized to go further and actually initiate the process of dying—that they should, in effect, kill their patients. Others would extend this authorization still further by legalizing the co-operation in others' suicide.

There is a range of opinion, a continuum from the belief that attempts to preserve life should be made at all costs, to the view that ending the lives of certain people should be legalized and that co-operation in others' suicide should be legal.

In addition to the ethical issues, one major problem is that of defining 'certain people', those whose lives may legally be ended. I am writing this in the Netherlands, and on the continent of Europe the shadow of Hitler's policy of genocide seems longer and darker than in Britain. A major problem in the proposal to legalize co-operation in a person's suicide is that he or she might be subjected to unscrupulous pressure. The problem with legalizing an arrangement whereby active measures may be taken to end a person's life at their own request when they reach a certain medical or mental condition is that, when people suffer from serious disease, considerable changes in their attitudes may occur as their condition worsens; and by the time they reach the stipulated condition, they may not want to die.

People who press for the legalization of euthanasia, either by putting an end to life or by co-operation in suicide, include those who are themselves disabled and suffering; other people who are in contact with suffering people; and yet others who base their arguments solely on theoretical principles. When we meet a disabled person who wants to commit suicide, or who wants to be put to death if physically unable to do it single-handed, we need to ask ourselves to what extent *we* are guilty that such people find their lives not worth living. Have we as members of the community done all that is within our power to make their lives worth living? Have we, in de Juvenel's terms, provided or enlisted the help of 'more powerful others' who might be able to master the pain, alleviate the distress, enrich the present life and modify the future—all of which are dominating for the sufferers? When we meet relatives who ask for euthanasia to be used, it is often the case that they feel themselves to be totally helpless observers and that they cannot tolerate the other person's suffering. They themselves need help.

The third policy of care is that of assisting the severely disabled baby, child or adult to live as rich a life as possible, with control of pain, breathlessness and nausea; and to die a natural death. Dame Cicely Saunders in her pioneer work with chronically sick and dying children and adults has shown that pain can be fully controlled in almost all people without affecting their personalities. This is achieved by the careful selection and combination of drugs to suit each person individually and, even more important, by the psychological aspects of the way in which the care is given, by the emotional aspects of the environment of care. Her policy may be summed up in her words: 'Depth in time is more important than length.'[6] In yet another aspect of the lives of disabled people, in the time of their dying, the quality of their personal relationships is of paramount importance.

Perhaps I should state where I stand personally in this debate. The words that I wrote fifteen years ago, when I described how I hoped doctors would treat people with disabling impairments or those who were dying, how they would treat me and those dear to me, still apply:

> I would hope that attempts would be made to resuscitate or treat a dying person if there was a chance of recovery from an acute illness but I would hope that heroic surgery or active resuscitation measures would not be undertaken in a person dying from a chronic illness, especially if they thereby prolonged existence as opposed to life. I do not believe that it is wrong or contrary to Christian principles to allow a person to die under these circumstances, a view put forward by a study group of the Church Assembly Board for Social Responsibility. They consider that it breaks no unalterable Christian law if, on the principle of loving his neighbour as himself, a doctor allows a patient to die. This policy carries with it the responsibility to give all needed care and attention to relieve physical pain and discomfort, and to recognize the dying person's emotional needs and meet them as far as possible. . . .
>
> When a person suffers from a chronic static or slowly progressive disease I do not think that his life should be ended, even at his own request. . . . If we decline to assist such people to die we have the moral responsibility to ensure that we help to make their lives as rich as possible.[7]

My attitude may be summarized in the aphorism written last century by Arthur Hugh Clough in 'The Latest Decalogue'.

Thou shalt not kill; but need'st not strive
Officiously to keep alive.

All these situations in which a decision about life or death must be made are distressing and the principles involved are of fundamental importance, but they need to be seen in the wide context of disabled people. For every child who is untreated and cared for until he or she dies, there are more who are treated: for every adult who wants to die, there are more who want to live. I am reminded of a woman I read about in the *Guardian* some years ago. She broke her neck in an accident and was severely disabled, but by using modern equipment she achieved considerable independence which she prized highly. She said: 'Every morning, when I wake up, I think — another day, and I've made it.'

Religious and philosophical questions

The central question, and the one encountered most frequently, is 'Why me?' — Why was I born disabled? Why have I become disabled? Why was my child born disabled? Why has my child/husband/wife become disabled?

Congenital disability. A legacy of the Puritan era lingers in some quarters in the association of sex with sin. As parents cast around to find a philosophical explanation for their child's congenital disability, they may wonder whether they are being punished for having had pre-marital or extra-marital sexual experience, or whether they may unknowingly have committed some other sexual 'sin'. (I am not referring to the possibilities of venereal infection, as this is usually excluded by modern ante-natal care.) Sometimes there is mutual recrimination as each parent blames the other, or blames the other's family for its 'unhealthy' medical history.

As congenitally disabled children grow up and become aware of their disabled condition, they may blame their parents for having brought them into the world like that. If they resent their disability, they may, by association, develop resentment of their parents also. There is great variation in the ways in which parents and growing children react, but these attitudes may be encountered.

Simple medical information which demonstrates the absence of personal responsibility may help to assuage the sense of guilt and the blame, although some individuals may need extensive counselling to gain this freedom. All the same, the metaphysical question 'why' remains as part of the whole problem of suffering.

Acquired disability. When able-bodied children or adults become disabled by accident or disease they often feel that they are in some way responsible through something they have, or have not, done—as Murray Parkes showed (p. 69) with the men and women who had had a limb amputated. Concurrently, they usually blame someone else as well. While they do not blame those treating them for their initial loss of able-bodiedness, it is not unusual for disabled people to blame medical staff for allegedly exacerbating their disability or for failing to improve their condition adequately.

Relatives, even more frequently, feel responsible for the disability, particularly the parents of children. It has been suggested that when people believe that their disability, or that of a relative, is retribution for a sin they have committed in the past, they respond with feelings of guilt which can lead to depression. If the disability is felt to be unfair, it may cause anger and resentment. If it is felt to be pointless and purposeless, it may give rise to anxious agitation.[8]

Mrs James (ch. 2) became disabled and experienced premature dependence. We can compare this early loss of able-bodiedness and the associated feelings of bereavement with the bereavement following the early death of a young husband or wife. Murray Parkes writes: 'Untimely death casts doubts on the "reasonable expectations" on which we base our lives.' We all do dangerous things, such as crossing busy roads or travelling by car or leaving a piece of frayed carpet unrepaired, but the knowledge that accidents are statistically rare helps us to feel that we are protected from disaster. Murray Parkes points out that a major bereavement shakes one's confidence in this sense of security, and the thought that a loved person's death was accidental is unacceptable because it makes us feel so impotent.[9] Perhaps there is another parallel here. When a person is disabled in an accident or by the 'accident' of congenital or acquired disability, his or her grief for the loss of able-bodiedness may be complicated by similar feelings of impotence: by the feeling of being dominated.

When disabled people experience this emotional suffering, their physical suffering may be increased. Anything that affects a person's tranquillity lowers their pain threshold, so that they experience more severe pain: and it also increases their physical symptoms.[10] This is another example of emotional factors affecting the body.

Sometimes the question is not so much 'Why me?' as 'Why now?'. Miss Kristine Gibbs is a social worker in her early thirties. At the age of twenty-six she was physically disabled by a second cerebral haemorrhage (a stroke) and lost her power of speech. She has recorded her experiences and feelings during the years of rehabilitation:

> The whole situation was so confusing. It seemed I was being told so many things by God which I could only half grasp. I had believed He had intended me to be appointed to the post in the hospital, particularly once I started to see results. Was this illness His way of removing a failure? I squirmed inside, churning over recent events, looking for where I had gone wrong. It was not difficult to find negative incidents, but there was the indisputable evidence that perceptive relationships on my unit had been improving since my arrival.[11]

I have found that disabled people and their families are able, out of their physical and emotional suffering, to face these questions squarely. When they raise a question, directly or indirectly, they want an answer or a discussion that does justice to their condition: the easy answer or the glib reply is not for them. Sometimes the best help is for counsellors to acknowledge that they have no answer, that they also do not know why.

Varieties of religious response. Disabled people with a Christian background react in different ways. For some, their Christian belief creates additional problems as they find it very difficult to reconcile their disability with the existence of a God of love, and relatives of disabled people may feel the same.

Mrs Kitty Carpenter suffered from a locomotor impairment which made activity and travel difficult. In her late thirties, she developed a potentially lethal internal impairment for which she had prolonged treatment. She experienced severe side-effects from the treatment but she persevered and obtained many months free of trouble. She wrote to me about her illness and her treatment, and about her physical and emotional distress. She had no self-pity that a disabled woman should have this further suffering, but she wrote: 'Where is God in all this? I try to have faith in God but it is very difficult.'

Mrs Carpenter had no contact with the Church but had been brought up in the Church of England as a child. She retained her memories of faith with a strong ethical component and a strong sense of justice which were her guidelines in her actions and in her relationships with people.

I wrote to her about John V. Taylor's concept of the Holy Spirit as the Go-Between-God who is knowable in the relationships between people.[12] I told her I believed that in all the relationships which she had with people who were trying to help her — her family, the doctors and therapists — the Holy Spirit was present and active in their helping. This met her need: she understood and believed that God in the form of the Holy Spirit was with her in all her suffering.

Some months later, her illness started to progress and the specialist pressed her to have further treatment. She was warned that there was no guarantee that the treatment would be effective but that without it she would not live longer than six months. She was appalled to learn that she faced further disability and pain and that further treatment, with all its side-effects, was necessary. She discussed the problem with her family who said that they would support her in whatever decision she made. She also discussed it with her general practitioner who promised to care for her at home whether or not she had the treatment, and to ensure that she remained free from pain.

I was abroad at the time, but she telephoned me across the North Sea. She talked for half an hour, weighing up the problematical advantages of further treatment, with the associated distress, against the possibility of a few months of happy life with her family. I listened, and spoke only to ask questions to clarify certain issues: I did this for her benefit rather than for mine. Eventually I said, 'I think, Kitty, that you have already made up your mind.' She replied, 'Yes, I think I have. I knew you were the person to help me, and I needed to hear myself say it. And I wanted to know that you thought it all right to refuse treatment.'

Shortly after this, I was in England and I went to see her at home. She was clearly very ill but was relaxed and calm, taking medicine from her general practitioner which relieved her pain and did not affect her personality. She told me of her plans to move into a front bedroom so that, if she later became confined to bed, she would have a prettier outlook and would be able to watch the children on the green. Apart from this, she did not overtly refer to her coming death or to our shared faith, but we tacitly accepted them as the background to our meeting. We had a happy afternoon, sitting on the sofa, reminiscing about the things we had done together and the people we knew. When I left, we promised to meet again in the summer if she were still alive. She died peacefully in her new bedroom later that spring.[13]

Kitty would have been embarrassed and sceptical if anyone had called her a religious woman, but I think that some words by Bill Kyle are relevant to her:

A healthy religious attitude is far more important than a bagful of beliefs. I can *say* 'I believe' about anything, but my *attitude* to life is the result, the sum, of my whole personality.

'A religious attitude' means having reverence for the whole of life. It means striving to find true meaning and purpose in life. It means being convinced that, at the heart of the universe, there is a Creator who is Love. It means to live the whole of life in a sacramental way. It means a commitment to transform the world around us, so that we can see the signs and the appearance of God's Kingdom here and now.[14]

Some committed Christians feel very strongly that God directly influences events, and orders the whole course of their lives. This belief calls for acceptance and patience and full co-operation in God's plan for them. Kristine Gibbs has written:

During the previous few years I had become less scared of letting God take the initiative, without trying to intervene. It was very difficult: I kept finding that, however hard I tried, I was continually butting in. Too uncertain; too little faith.[15]

Miss Gibbs ends her book with this paragraph:

When this book was begun, I could hardly put two sentences together. Now, five years later, I am writing fluently and, apart from the occasional dyspraxic mistake, my speech is normal. Why should the extent and quality of my survival have been so profound? My progress stems from the knowledge that I am not my own, but Christ's. I knew that from the mustard seed of my faith, God could create a tree. In the context of His strength, my vulnerability and the ridicule of an agnostic public become irrelevant. The struggle continues, but in Christ its heart is peace. This book is a tribute to the small group of people who had the courage to share in the vision of survival and rehabilitation. It is a testimony not to the strength of man, but to the wisdom, power and infinite love of God.[16]

While I respect the beliefs of people who feel this way, I find it increasingly difficult to believe in the concept of a God who is both all-powerful *and* all-loving. As I try to reconcile my professional and personal life experience with official Christian doctrine, I feel that I have to make a choice between these two attributes.

On the continent of Europe, the horrific treatment of the Jews in Auschwitz is still exercising Jewish and Christian theological writers and, as a woman who calls herself a Christian, I cannot stand outside these issues. If I have to make a choice, I would choose for love rather than power. This belief calls for a more active co-operation with God, more of a partnership, albeit a very unequal and dependent partnership.

Some years ago, the playwright Dennis Potter spoke about the freedom of man as being something given. At that time he was disabled by a painful and rare form of arthritic disease. He said:

I have the sense that the world is made every day, second
by second, minute by minute, and we, living in this world,
give back some of that initial gift, minute by minute,
second by second; that even the most trivial choice can
have awesome consequences; that the way we live in
relation to other people is a continual tension of choice;
that that choice has its origin in a loving creation; and that
that loving creation is in continual battle with and tension
with and in obvious opposition to the misery, cruelty and
crudity of an imperfect world that we have to endure and
live in and do battle with.[17]

I find myself much in sympathy with Dennis Potter's belief
that 'that loving creation is in continual battle with and
tension with and in obvious opposition to' the suffering and
evil in the world. I feel that we have the choice to join with
God in the battle and to share the tension. It seems to me that
something of this concept of active partnership underlies the
description which Audrey Shepherd gave of her response as a
Christian to her disability. Her essay was written fifteen
years ago, at the age of forty. I must be careful not to interpret
her words in the light of my present concerns, so I quote them
in full:

For me, disability means learning to live a double life! At
the same time as accepting my present limitations and
seeking to take a new place in the community, I must work
with God for wholeness, and this is done secretly, in the
heart. 'Trying' and 'fighting' can make a person hard,
determined to accept help from nobody, cold and arrogant.
The paradox is that nevertheless one must 'try' and 'fight',
quietly, faithfully, gently and patiently. For the Christian
this means that the trying is done in the strength of Jesus,
plodding along in his steps, for it is the Father's will that
we should be made whole, as individuals and as a
community.[18]

References

1 Campling, J. (ed.), *Images of Ourselves.* Routledge & Kegan Paul
1981. Quoted in *Community Care,* 1 October, 1981.

2 Morgan, Margaret R., paper presented at the International Symposium on 'Family and Society' of the International Cerebral Palsy Society, Paris 1972.
3 Chalmers, R., 'Victim Invicta', in Hunt, P. (ed.), *Stigma: The Experience of Disability.* G. Chapman 1966.
4 'Matters of life and death', in the *Guardian Weekly.* 15 November 1981, p. 10.
5 Garrad, J., 'The right to die', in *Journal of Medical Social Work.* Vol. 20 (1968), no. 11, pp. 327-30.
6 Saunders, C., in Schoenberg, B. *et al.* (eds.), *Psychosocial Aspects of Terminal Care* (Columbia University Press 1972), pp. 275-89.
7 Garrad, J., op. cit., p. 328.
8 Muir Gray, J. A., 'Caring for religious aspects of disability', in *The Times.* 7 February 1981.
9 Murray Parkes, C., *Bereavement. Studies of Grief in Adult Life* (Tavistock Publications 1972), p. 85.
10 Muir Gray, J. A., op. cit.
11 Gibbs, K., *Only One Way Up* (Darton, Longman & Todd 1981), p. 21.
12 Taylor, J. V., *The Go-Between God.* Mowbray 1972.
13 The example of Mrs Kitty Carpenter (a fictional name) is included with the knowledge of her husband, as a tribute to a woman who helped many people during her life; and in the hope that others may be strengthened by the manner of her dying.
14 Kyle, W., *The Wholeness of Man* (The Westminster Pastoral Foundation Booklet 1980), p. 1.
15 Gibbs, K., op. cit., p. 21.
16 ibid., pp. 167-8.
17 Potter, D., quoted by Craig, M., *The Listener.* Vol. 106 (December 1981), no. 2741, p. 818.
18 Shepherd, A., 'One body', in Hunt, P., op. cit., p. 66.

Suggestions for reading

Baelz, P., *Ethics and Belief.* Sheldon Press 1977.
Clark, B., *Whose Life Is It Anyway?* Amber Lane Press 1978. (play)
Dominian, J., *Proposals for a New Sexual Ethic.* Darton, Longman & Todd 1977.
Gardner, R. F. R., *Abortion: The Personal Dilemma.* Paternoster 1972.
Hick, J., *Evil and the God of Love.* Fontana 1968.
Meddoff, M., *Children of a Lesser God.* Amber Lane Press 1982. (play)
Trowell, H., *The Unfinished Debate on Euthanasia.* SCM Press 1973.

EIGHT

Dying and grieving and helping

It is a platitude to say that we all must die. We all know it but the majority of people prefer not to think about it or to talk about it. But for all of us death is part of life, and every day we risk an accident which may be fatal. Yet my studies showed that, for physically disabled people, the chances of death at any age are five times greater than for people of the same ages in their community. The reasons for this difference are complex, but for some people the nature of their impairment may be lethal, or they may be more susceptible to infections or to other secondary impairments. For them, therefore, death is even more a part of life. But just as able-bodied people do not think or talk about their death all the time, neither do disabled people: but they, or more frequently their relatives, speak of it more readily than able-bodied people. Paul Hunt (ch. 3) wrote: 'Involuntarily we walk — or more often sit — in the valley of the shadow of death.'

Clergy and others engaged in pastoral care with disabled people and their families will therefore meet increased numbers of dying people and bereaved relatives, and so they must be prepared for meeting people in situations of dying, death and bereavement.

Dying and helping

When a child or adult is dying and has the company of his or her family, friends and professional staff, only one person is dying but all are, or can be, helping. It is this concept of mutual interdependence that I want to emphasize in this chapter.

When people are dying they often pass through a number of stages in their emotional response which can be considered as an elaboration of the phases in the response to a crisis.

108

These phases merge and overlap, and different people may react in a different order.[1]

In the culture of western Europe, death is largely a taboo subject, an attitude which tends to heighten people's fear of dying themselves and of the death of others. When people are told that they are dying, or they come to realize it, they usually experience a great shock during which they tend to deny the fact: and this denial may isolate them from their family and helpers. The dying person's wish for denial must be respected, but people should show, by availability and non-verbal signs, that they are willing to talk should the dying person wish to open up a little.

As dying people come to realize their situation they may become very angry, especially if they are young and feel that their death is far too early. Rosalind Chalmers (ch. 6) has described her reactions:

> This polio, which we had feared for our children, was certainly unpleasant but only temporary. Then when I lay gasping in hospital I suddenly realized I was dying, and was at first very angry indeed. It seemed, when there was so much to see and to do, to be entirely the wrong moment to die.[2]

In particular, disabled people who have achieved independence in their lives may be frightened by this form of domination. They may react with anger to the people caring for them whom they may see as another form of control. People's anger should be accepted as a sign of distress, and they should be given the opportunity for expressing it and talking about the reasons for it. Those who bottle up their anger and resentment often find it much harder to die.

A bargaining stage may follow in which the person may try to propitiate God or Fate or the powerful professionals: and this is usually replaced by a great sense of loss—loss of things in the past and present and the impending loss of a future. I think that when Kitty Carpenter and I were reminiscing about the past, she was taking leave of it. If people are depressed at this time, they need to know that others understand. Words are not always necessary. It is a time when the familiar adage 'Don't just stand there; do something!' should be reversed: 'Don't do anything; just be there!' In such periods of quiet companionship, perhaps holding hands, the person may begin to speak about his deepest feelings, or ask his philosophical or religious questions, or ask for prayer. Physical contact, the sense of touch, becomes increasingly important to the dying person when the deepest communication may be without words.

The period of acceptance which usually follows may develop into a period of personal growth, of deeper self-knowledge and closer relationships with those of the family, friends and helpers who are accompanying the individual in his or her dying.

During all this time, the relatives usually need help or the support of knowing that help is available if they want it. Relatives may experience many of the same stages as the dying person, but their reaction will depend on whether the death is felt to be untimely or unexpected, or long expected or a release. If they can be helped concurrently with the dying person, they may be ready emotionally to meet that person's emotional needs. It should be remembered that if the dying person or relatives are members of the helping professions, they may need the same help as others but may not ask for it, thinking that they are expected to cope professionally by themselves.

When the dying person and the relatives are able to meet each other's emotional needs, they may all experience greater closeness and be able to help each other with their preparatory grieving.

Mr Thomas was a business executive in his middle fifties; he was dying in hospital. He was restless and clearly distressed, although he tried hard to hide this. When I went to the ward to see him, he at once told me that he knew he was very ill and he thought that he might be dying. If he was, he knew that his wife would have been told; in which case he also wished to know. He said that throughout their married life they had always shared their sorrows as well as their joys, and he did not want his dying and his death to be any exception. I told the physician and he spoke privately with Mr Thomas. He told him that, as far as could be known, it was unlikely that he would recover. Mr Thomas became much calmer. During his last weeks, his wife was with him on the ward for very long periods and they both gave the impression of quiet serenity.

It is worth noting that the policy of this physician was always to talk about dying if the patient requested it: but he never said definitely that the patient was dying. This was partly because any doctor can be wrong, but mainly because he considered it important to leave some hope for the person to cling to if he was not ready to face the full truth. In Macquarrie's words, he did not foreclose the future but left the possibility of an open space ahead.

The next example shows that the attitudes of a dying disabled person may change, and emphasizes how the period of dying can be a time of profound personal relationships.

Mr Peter King, a physicist aged about thirty, suffered from an internal impairment which progressed so that he became disabled after marriage. His wife was in her mid-twenties but they had no children, as Mr King became impotent. I had known them both for about a year, and had talked with them in their home and in the hospital, before Mr King was readmitted to hospital for terminal care.

Mr King knew his diagnosis and he knew that he was dying. Although he did not discuss his dying or his death, he discussed with me what advance arrangements he could make for his young wife 'when she would be alone'. (This is often a source of comfort for a dying person.) Mr King was being nursed in a single room and on one occasion when I called in to see him, his wife was there also. We three had one of our many talks together and then Mr King suddenly asked: 'Can you help me to get a job when I am better?' I was taken completely by surprise and answered, 'Well—yes.' Mr King repeated insistently, 'You *can?*' I felt trapped between his insistence and my inadvertent and inappropriate reply; and, unable to think quickly enough, I replied, 'Yes, if that is what you want.' That was the turning point. The conversation came to an ambiguous end and, from then on, my relationship with Mr King wilted.

After he had died, I kept in touch with Mrs King during the period when widowed people are particularly vulnerable. She told me 'how curiously happy' she and her husband had been during the weeks when he was dying; and that he had told her she was the only person who did not lie to him or put him off with half truths. I remembered our conversation about finding work when he was better: I realized that he had been testing me out and that I had failed him. A more helpful reply to his question might have been 'Yes, if you think that will be possible.' This would have enabled him to continue his denial of death if he wished, but it would also have left the way open for a discussion of getting better, or not getting better, or of dying. This was probably what Mr King wanted. Previously he had not been ready to talk about his dying or his death as it affected him, only as it affected his wife. When he was ready to talk about himself, I did not recognize my cue. It was an early and painful experience from which I learned a lot.

Members of the family, as well as professional staff, are not always able to meet the dying person's emotional needs by being available and willing to talk about dying when he or she wants to. People may avoid contact with a dying person or keep relationships on a superficial level: this has been called the bereavement of the dying. People do this because, consciously or not, the subject of death is too distressing because they have not come to terms with their own mortality.

People experienced in the care of dying children emphasize the importance of life enrichment for them during their last months or weeks, and the importance of the parents being involved in as many aspects of their care as possible. This is very important for the child and the parents. Children are often better able to face the possibility of dying than adults expect, but, understandably, parents usually need much support to enable them to maintain an open and close relationship with their dying child. Experiences with large numbers of dying children have confirmed that they and their parents have been able to mature during this stressful time.[3]

Macquarrie emphasizes that nothing can minimize the significance of death, but he says that in some way it is death that makes a meaningful life possible.[4]

For death sets a boundary to life, and makes it possible for a human life to constitute a finite whole. On this view, life could be compared to a piece of music. If that piece of music just went on and on indefinitely, it would have no

form or meaning or beauty. It derives its form and beauty
by working out its material in a finite temporal pattern. So
too, a human life, lived in death awareness, develops its
meaning from the responsible deployment of its resources
in face of the end.

Macquarrie concedes that no *tour de force* can convert death
into a good, and that for every person whose death is
meaningful 'there are many more whose deaths are senseless,
wasteful and frustrating'. He continues:

> Yet the fact that in some ways death is redeemable and can
> even contribute to the quality of a life suggests that hope is
> not entirely cancelled by death and that hope can persist
> even in the face of death. Just what that hope might be is
> not clear. . . . Yet death has not quenched hope. Unclear
> though the hope may be, there has always been a hope that
> has stood out against death, and in face of the total threat
> of death there has arisen the total hope that even death can
> be transformed and made to contribute to life.

If the dying person and his or her relative can share the
resolution of life in this way, the parting may be easier for
them both. Sometimes the dying person reaches this stage
first and can help his or her relative to share, but sometimes a
third person must give the relative this help. One dying
woman was deeply distressed because her husband could not
face the thought of losing her, and she asked a counsellor to
help because she said that she could not die until she knew
that he was ready to let her go. When he had been helped to
recognize her coming death and to share the parting with her,
she relaxed and died peacefully.[5]

Erich Lindemann wrote the early classical studies of grief.
When he was diagnosed as suffering from a fatal illness, he
recorded his experiences and feelings while he was dying. In
the posthumous publication, the editor writes: 'In facing the
stress of his terminal illness Erich Lindemann offers himself
as a living example of the inter-relationship of patient and
helping agents in mutual understanding and coping. . . .
There is no hierarchy of roles or linear sequence of action, but
a dynamic interchange of realities in which patient, therapist
and family *share* . . . the task and the consequences.'[6]

Some dying people, particularly those who have been fighters all their lives may need permission to die, permission to stop fighting, to relax and live the last part of their lives in calmness. This was what Kitty Carpenter meant when she told me on the telephone: 'I needed to know that you thought it all right to refuse treatment.'

When people have no relatives or friends with whom to share their need for love and companionship when dying, volunteers have a special contribution to make. One parish in England has a Good Neighbour Scheme for the express purpose of providing companionship and support to dying people and their families.

This kind of intensely personal help makes great emotional demands on the helpers. Cicely Saunders has shown how often helpers draw strength from the people they are helping, and emphasizes this reciprocal nature of the relationship. She shows, too, how important is the support that helpers can give each other when they are working in an open and sharing environment.[7]

The importance to the dying person, and thus also to his or her relative, of this mutual understanding and closeness is movingly clear in a letter written by a Cockney woman to her husband shortly before she died in hospital.[8]

> Dear Alf, I seen you last night in my dream. O my dear I cried at waking up. What a silly girl you been and got. The pain is bad this morning but I laugh at the sollum cloks of the sisters and the sawbones. I can see they think I am booked but they don't know what has befalen between you and me. How could I die and leave my Dear. I spill my medecin this morning thinking of my dear. Hopeing this finds you well. No more now from yours truly Liz.

Perhaps this endorses the words attributed to Arnold Toynbee: 'Love cannot save life from death, but it can fulfil life's purpose.'

Grieving and helping

No one ever told me that grief felt so like fear. I am not afraid, but the sensation is like being afraid. The same fluttering in the stomach, the same restlessness, the yawning. I keep on swallowing.

At other times it feels like being mildly drunk, or concussed. There is a sort of invisible blanket between the world and me. I find it hard to take in what anyone says. Or perhaps hard to want to take it in. It is so uninteresting. Yet I want the others to be about me. I dread the moments when the house is empty. If only they would talk to one another and not to me.[9]

These two paragraphs were written in his diary by C. S. Lewis, following the death of his wife after a long illness during which they had grieved together and shared their religious beliefs, hopes and doubts. The extracts give in a nutshell the three principal needs of bereaved people: help in making contact with other people and in doing practical tasks; companionship; privacy. I have discussed earlier the main characteristics of bereavement in relation to the onset of disability. In this chapter I mention those points to which I have found it useful to be alert.

Some bereaved relatives want to see the body, others definitely do not and others are ambivalent. Except in cases of severe mutilation, most people look peaceful after death owing to the relaxation of the facial muscles, and this can give comfort to relatives. Seeing the body also clearly marks the end of one stage of life for the survivors and the start of a new one: this time-boundary is often helpful in starting healthy grieving and the readjustment to a new way of life. Some people find comfort in physical contact and people should be able to cry freely if they wish: some men may need permission to cry—they may need reassurance that men as well as women cry in grief. Those people who are hesitant and slightly fearful of seeing the body may be helped by the offer: 'Shall I come with you? Shall I hold your hand?' I have found that this offer is often gratefully accepted by adult men and women: and it is particularly important with bereaved children.

The 'sort of invisible blanket' makes it difficult for some people to deal with practical matters, especially funeral arrangements. It is important that the family members should be warned of the stressful moments in a cremation service or in an interment, as relatives can be deeply distressed by the experience when this warning is omitted. Rituals associated with dying, death or burial are of great value: they stimulate the expression of grief in a way which is recognized and approved in the people's culture, and they help to focus grief and minimize the risk of a diffuse, generalized anxiety. Differences of ritual among people of different cultures are very important and helpers should acquaint themselves with these.[10]

Many bereaved people need to talk repeatedly about the dead person's last days or hours, and particularly about the moment of death if they witnessed it. By contrast, some are so numbed that they need help to start their grief work. If the rituals of the funeral do not help, the use of photographs may be helpful, particularly if the bereaved person is distressed to find that he or she cannot visualize the lost person. Photographs provide the opportunity for the bereaved person to 'pain through' former shared events and to talk to the helper about them.

Most bereaved people experience some sense of guilt in relation to the person's death or about some aspect of their lives together. This may sometimes be the most stressful and long-lasting emotion. People usually find it a great personal relief to be told that in all grieving there is normally a sense of guilt, as this knowledge eliminates the feeling that they are uniquely guilty and assuages their sense of personal responsibility.

C. S. Lewis noted the physical changes which a bereaved person may experience. I have quoted Murray Parkes's description of these and his warning of the increased illness and the increased death rate among people during the first six months of widowhood. Helpers therefore need to be alert to signs of ill-health in the bereaved person and, perhaps more importantly, to help him or her follow a daily routine which does not further increase the risk of illness.

At the same time, it is desirable that the bereaved person be helped to recognize that he or she has a future. In all situations of change, there is an element of loss and an element of gain: sometimes the one predominates, sometimes the other. If the bereaved person can be helped to find some small element of gain, something positive in the new situation, it may provide the starting point for looking to the future with hope. It may, as Macquarrie has said, provide the 'open road' before the person along which he or she can choose to move.

References

1 Kubler-Ross, E., *On Death and Dying.* Social Science Paperbacks (Tavistock Publications) 1973.
2 Chalmers, R., in Hunt, P., *Stigma: The Experience of Disability* (G. Chapman 1966), p. 20.
3 Morse, J., 'The goal of life enhancement for a fatally ill child', in *Children.* Vol. 17 (March—April 1970), no. 2.
4 Macquarrie, J., *Christian Hope* (Mowbray 1978), pp. 19-20.
5 Kubler-Ross, E., op. cit., p. 104.
6 Lindemann, E., *Beyond Grief, Studies in Crisis Intervention* (Jason Aronson 1979), pp. 239 and 230.
7 Saunders, C., 'A therapeutic community', in Schoenberg, B., *et al.* (eds.), *Psychosocial Aspects of Terminal Care* (Columbia University Press 1972), p. 275.
8 De la Mare, W. (compiler), *An Anthology of Love.* Faber & Faber (out of print).
9 Lewis, C. S., *A Grief Observed* (Faber Paperback Editions 1971), p. 7.
10 Speck, P. W., *Loss and Grief in Medicine* (Baillière Tindall 1978), part iii.

Suggestions for reading

Kubler-Ross, E.; Lewis, C. S.; Lindemann, E.; Murray Parkes, C.; Schoenberg, B. *et al.* (eds.): all as above. Also:
Burton, Lindy (ed.), *The Care of the Child Facing Death.* Routledge & Kegan Paul 1974.
Cartwright, A., Hockey, L., and Anderson, J. A., *Life before Death.* Routledge & Kegan Paul 1973. The needs and provision of care in the last year of life, based on a study of 700 people aged fifteen and over.
Hinton, J., *Dying.* Pelican 1967.
Marris, P., *Loss and Change.* Routledge & Kegan Paul 1974. Especially the introduction and ch. 2. Also ch. 5, 'Mourning and the Projection of Ambivalence'.
Pincus, L., *Death and the Family. The Importance of Mourning.* Faber & Faber 1976.
Speck, P., and Ainsworth-Smith, I., *Letting Go: Caring for the Dying and Bereaved.* SPCK 1982.
Toynbee, A. *et al., Man's Concern with Death.* Hodder & Stoughton 1969. Essays by members of different professions and from different standpoints.

NINE

Some principles of helping

In this chapter I describe some methods which I have found useful when offering help to disabled people and their families, and which can be used in pastoral care: then I consider some policies of care.

Some methods of helping

Help in a crisis

The aim of helping in a crisis is to assist the person to weather the storm. The most important feature of this help is the timing of the offer to help. Mr O'Reilly (ch. 2) was able to use my help mainly because the offer was made at the crucial time — when he was still reeling under the shock of becoming disabled. If we think in terms of the crisis model, he was in the phase of disorganization: in terms of the whole person model, he was in the phase of disequilibrium. The help I was able to give him enabled him to reorganize his thoughts and feelings, to get them in perspective, to regain his equilibrium. Mr Roberts (ch. 2) did not receive help at this stage of his illness. When he was admitted to hospital and I visited him, he had passed the time when he would have been receptive of help, albeit perhaps grudgingly. He had achieved a measure of reorganization and equilibrium, in which the paramount characteristics of depression and resentment were self-defeating.

The kind of help offered should be related to the nature of the person's emotional reaction to the crisis and to the immediate practical needs. With some people, one careful interview may be all that is required to steady them up so that they can deal with the crisis by their own resources. With other people, the need for help may spread over many weeks as they move slowly through the different phases which are characteristic of the response to a crisis. The helper therefore has to be flexible and prepared to adjust his or her help to the person's changing needs. Help may range from being alongside, to helping people express anxiety or anger verbally as this often relieves the emotions; or to assisting people to take some appropriate action themselves, because the feeling of getting something done often relieves anxiety. However, some very anxious people react by overactivity as a means of warding off depression. Such overactivity is often ineffective and this failure increases the anxiety. Others react to a crisis by disbelief of such intensity that they deny the existence of the crisis — it is too awful to face. They need much patient understanding and help in facing up to the situation; and companionship and support as they begin to do so, because they may then become overtly anxious or depressed. Thus anxiety may stimulate a person to activity or it may be inhibitory. Each person can tolerate a certain amount of anxiety and this tolerance level is different for different people. Amounts of anxiety below this level are stimulating to thought and action, but amounts above it are inhibiting.

During the phase when people are receptive of help, they are particularly vulnerable as they can easily succumb to pressure to do as the helper, or the family, thinks fit. This places a great responsibility on helpers for assessing their own part in the situation and maybe for protecting the person from undue pressure from others. This applies particularly with bereaved people who may feel that the future holds nothing more for them, and so may readily part with possessions, which they later regret doing. I found it helpful to advise bereaved people whose family wanted some possessions, to make a list of the requests for gifts and to defer a decision until later when they were more settled.

Throughout the different phases of the crisis, the helpers' object is to help people deal with the crisis themselves. Helpers may need to give information, advice, encouragement and support, as well as counsel over the things that are causing distress. As the aim of the help is to enable the person to become as independent as possible, the helpers should decide with the person when the time is appropriate for them to withdraw from active help, while remaining available if needed. Help that is too prolonged may be undermining and delay a person's emotional recovery and resumption of personal responsibility: while premature withdrawal may be interpreted as desertion and is thus harmful.

Long-term help

In the parable of the man who fell among thieves,[1] it could be said that the Samaritan gave crisis help and that the innkeeper gave long-term help. Thus if problems persist beyond the end of the crisis, long-term help starts where crisis help ends. With disabled people and their families, the goal or goals of long-term help vary with the severity of the person's disability and the nature of the impairment. Help may be needed to support the family through a bad patch lasting several months, or it may be to help the person and family 'to go on going on' over many years. In this situation, the needs of the caring relative become very important and he, or more usually she, may need help in his or her own right. The disability and the disabled person should be seen in the context of the family as a whole, so that care may be given to meet the needs of the family unit. Caring relatives may need someone to take some of the load off their shoulders, but may feel too guilty to share the care; while sometimes the relative becomes very possessive of the disabled person and is too jealous to allow anyone else to help in caring. This may apply particularly when the care includes intimate and personal attention such as washing, toilet and menstrual care and feeding. (This component of care is now sometimes described as tending, to distinguish it from less physical forms of care.[2]) During tending, a strong emotional bond may develop between the helper and the person owing to repeated physical contacts. Some disabled people become selfish or manipulative and play on the helper's jealousy, so there may be a need for counselling over problems of personal relationships before any practical and material help can be given.

It is in long-term help that the concept of reciprocity is very important, linking up with the earlier discussion of mature dependence. I read somewhere (and cannot trace the source) of a severely disabled man who needed considerable tending from his wife and who was confined to his upstairs flat. But his attitude to life and to his disability was such that he was a great support to his wife: she used to say that she could not look after him without his help. Also, people from the housing estate who were in personal difficulties beat a track to his door to discuss their problems with him, and came away refreshed and strengthened. In this case the recipient of help was also a helper, both in his family circle and outside it.

Using the concept of loss

In all situations of change there is an element of gain and an element of loss: sometimes the one predominates, sometimes the other. When the loss predominates, help can be offered as to a bereaved person. This is an approach which is widely used in counselling and social work. I have discussed it in relation to the onset of disability and to the recognition of congenital disability. There are many medical and surgical conditions when a person has similar feelings of loss and bereavement.[3] The same conceptual approach may be used in understanding people's reactions to the loss of their home, for example, when they are admitted permanently to a home or hospital for disabled people; then they have the additional concurrent loss of personal independence.[4]

Many disabled people and their families have benefited from counselling based on this approach. However, some disabled people strongly object to it. One severely disabled man has written:

> Social work, like all other professions, has adopted the wrong model of disability. It's seen as a personal tragedy — a disaster that has to be adapted to by the individual disabled person. In support of this model, a rag-bag of concepts like grief, mourning, bereavement and loss have been borrowed from other areas in order to help impaired people adjust to their disability.
>
> Disabled people see it differently. For them, the problems don't stem from their individual impairments but from social organization. People in wheelchairs find it difficult to get into buildings with steps, not because of their individual limitations but because someone else chose to

put steps there in the first place. Many disabled people are unemployed, not because they don't want or are incapable of work, but because of the way production is organized or employers fail to give disabled people any sort of chance.[5]

This writer uses the structural model of disability in which disabled people's difficulties are attributed to the characteristics of the society in which they live and not to their disability or to their reaction to being disabled. According to this model, the disabled person does not need individual help with his or her difficulties, but needs assistance in obtaining improvements for disabled people generally and, if necessary, in altering the way in which society is organized so that these improvements can be made. For example, if the attitudes of society towards disabled people were different, there could be an amendment to the present legislation relating to suitable access facilities for disabled people to all public buildings. The amendment could make such provision obligatory instead of the present requirement to do so as far as possible. There would be public support for any extra costs even if the money came from funds earmarked for projects for able-bodied people. Or the existing regulation that 3 per cent of a workforce must consist of registered disabled people would be enforced, as it was when the legislation was passed during the Second World War with disabled ex-service men and women in mind. Such a practice would affect employers and trade unionists and, indeed, all employed people. During the 1940s this policy had public support: it is doubtful if it would be supported today.

These are the kinds of situation the author of the quotation refers to when he writes about the way in which society is organized, and calls for changes.

I do not think that the individual and structural approaches are mutually exclusive. Of the disabled people and their families who have benefited from counselling to help them with emotional problems, many have needed support in overcoming the attitudes of able-bodied employers or landlords, and help in overcoming material and practical difficulties. Their need for the one or the other kind of help often changes over time. Help that concentrates solely on effecting changes in society is as inappropriate, in my opinion, as help which concentrates on individual emotional problems to the exclusion of all else. The vehemence of the quotation serves to re-emphasize the importance of the helper remaining alert to recognition of the different attitudes, emotions and needs of disabled people, and flexible enough to co-operate with the disabled person in trying to meet them.

Enlisting other helpers

In pastoral care with physically disabled people and their families, clergy may recognize the existence of problems which they themselves cannot alleviate, whereas other professional or volunteer helpers with different skills or opportunities may be able to do so. In such situations it is in the best interests of the person for the clergy to enlist the aid of the most appropriate helper. This may frequently apply to practical and material needs. Without presenting a list of such likely needs, it can be said that requests for advice or help often relate to housing; schooling; further education or training and employment or finance; home care; recreation; temporary admission to a hostel, home or hospital to give the caring relative a break; or permanent admission. When suitable facilities are not available to meet these needs, everyone concerned comes up against obstacles resulting from the way in which society allocates its priorities, particularly in times of economic difficulty. In a later chapter I discuss the helpers' responsibilities in such situations.

Some policies of care

Prevention

In the discussion of Mary Hamilton's history (ch. 1), it was shown that people who suffer from a chronic impairment are at risk of becoming disabled. Many general practitioners now identify the people in their practice who are at risk, in order that they may give them special care in trying to prevent, or to delay, the onset of disability. Physically disabled people are at greater risk of developing some degree of emotional disturbance than are able-bodied people. So when the general practitioners and the local social workers know who are the disabled people in their area, it would be possible for them to co-operate with these people and their families to try to prevent the social and emotional difficulties which I have suggested may be important factors in the development of emotional disturbance. In this way they would reduce the risk of disabled people becoming emotionally disturbed. Unfortunately, with some splendid exceptions, these two professional groups do not pay much attention to this aspect of physical disability. I think that Christians, with their emphasis on the whole person, have a special part to play, with others who think like them, in the field of mental health. If clergy and parishioners accept this responsibility, it would be necessary for them to know the people in a parish who are at risk in order that preventive help may be offered. If helpers think that it would be inappropriate to make the first move and offer help, then they should ensure that the people who are at risk in this way know that help is available and that it is easy and acceptable to ask for it.

Prediction and planning ahead

When doctors assess the likely course of patients' illnesses and tell them the probable length and what the possible consequences are, they are using the policy of prediction. The medical profession is using this practice increasingly with physically disabled people, particularly in the Family Assessment Centres, so that the people and their families may plan ahead, making at least contingency plans. When Mary Hamilton was unable to continue with her fine work as a seamstress, she was told that her sight would probably continue to deteriorate. She trained for new work, as an audio typist, work which she could still do if she became blind—as she did. Such advance information is particularly important for disabled people who have family respon- sibilities. The object of planning ahead is to achieve as smooth a transition as possible from one style of life to another should it become necessary, and to try to create new gains to compensate for the losses.

Pastors have a part in helping disabled people and their families to cope with the advance information which is often distressing; and in helping them to decide on appropriate action and to carry it through. In order that such help may be effective, close co-operation may be necessary between pastors and other professionals, including doctors and social workers.

Styles of helping

However, if all the professionals co-operate in the best interests of the disabled person and family, they can defeat their own ends if they provide care or present the person with a solution to his or her problem. If they do this, they add another controlling factor to the person's dominating future. There are three main types of relationship between doctors and their patients,[6] and the descriptions also apply to other professionals and volunteers and the people whom they are helping. There is the activity - passivity relationship in which the helper is the active member while the individual is passive and receptive of help. In the guidance - co-operation relationship the helper makes recommendations, offers advice and encourages the individual to co-operate by giving relevant information. The third relationship is that of mutual participation in which the helper and the individual are equal partners; alternative aspects of the problem and alternative courses of action are jointly discussed and one is mutually selected and implemented.

These three types of relationship underlie different styles of helping. They are not discrete entities but three points on a continuum which runs from an authoritarian approach at one extreme to an egalitarian approach at the other. The helpers' style depends largely on temperament and on their perception of individual abilities, needs and preferences. The style of the person being helped depends, among other things, on temperament, on the nature of the impairment and the severity of the disability, and on their perception of the helpers' role. If, for example, people see their minister as a man of authority, they will think that they, as parishioners, should be receptive of his instructions. They would therefore consider it presumptuous to take an equal part in a discussion with him. Helpers must be flexible in their choice of approach in order to meet the different needs of different people; or the different needs of the same person at different times. It is only when the style of the helper and that of the person are compatible and mutually acceptable that counselling and other forms of help will be effective.

The more the individual and the helper are able to develop a relationship of mutual participation, the more will the individual be in control, so that such a relationship extends the area of the manageable future. In such a policy of care, the disabled person is a member of the caring team. This term implies that all the helpers are co-operating together and with the disabled person and his or her family in an open relationship. An example is the co-operation between Mary Hamilton, the physician in the diabetes clinic, and myself (ch. 1).

Community care

The membership of the caring team can be widened to include other helpers.

It has been pointed out that there are three aspects to the term community care: care *of* the community; care *in* the community; and care *by* the community.[7]

Care *of* the community describes the work of, for example, the Health Service or Social Services Department in providing their particular services in the area for which they are responsible. In order to do this satisfactorily, they must know what services are needed, how they can best be provided to the people who need them, and how priorities are to be set when there are insufficient resources to meet the needs of all the people.

In the context of the relationship between the Church and disabled people, care of the community means that the clergy know the numbers of disabled people in the area and understand their special needs. This enables them to know what aspects of pastoral care are particularly relevant for this group, so that they can work out the ways in which the Church can make its special contribution in the caring team.

Care *in* the community usually means that the disabled person is being cared for in his or her own home rather than in an institution. In addition to this concept of location, there is the connotation of relationships with other people, the concept of neighbourliness with the people who live nearby.

This is an aspect of city life which is often lacking and I have already discussed the relative isolation of many disabled people and their families. Audrey Shepherd has written:

> . . . there is an almost total lack of real community life. We have little sense of being bound up in one body, a body made up, not only of the healthy and the prosperous, the respectable and the successful but also of the old, the failures, the mentally ill, criminals, the physically handicapped, the misfits, the awkward squad. . . . And so there grows up a community without a heart . . . lacking life because it lacks wholeness.[8]

Perhaps the task of fostering real community life, of fostering wholeness, is an important part of the Church's pastoral care of the community and its care in the community in relation to disabled people.

Where this sense of community life does exist, people living in their own homes 'permeate' the institutions in their area when this is welcomed and, wherever possible, the residents in institutions visit the people's homes and go to the shops, etc. In this way, residents in hostels or homes for disabled people or hospitals take part in community life and may be said to be living in the community.

This leads to the third aspect, that of care *by* the community. Neighbourliness may be much more than gossip over the garden wall, although this is important. It is a relationship of mutual aid, as in the care of the disabled man (p. 121) who not only supported his wife in her care of him, but also helped neighbours with their difficulties, receiving in exchange the satisfaction of having a function in the community. Sometimes an informal organization may be needed, as when a group of women in a parish known to me arranged a rota among themselves to take a hot meal on Saturdays and Sundays to a disabled neighbour to whom the meals-on-wheels service delivered on weekdays only.

When the needs are more complex than in these examples, a more developed organization may be necessary. In many areas there are Good Neighbour Schemes, sometimes associated with churches, with local Councils of Social Service, or other voluntary organizations.

When people are helped by local residents, the distinction

between giver and recipient is blurred and the stigma of being a recipient is less. However, it can be difficult always to receive help from neighbours unless there is some reciprocity. When I first came to the Netherlands as a foreigner in The Hague, many years ago, I was able to offer some help to a neighbour when she was ill. Being an independent woman she found this difficult to accept, until she realized that she, in return, was giving me much needed friendship.

References

1 Luke 10.25f.
2 Parker, R. A., 'Tending and social policy', in Goldberg, E. M., and Hatch, S. (eds.), *A New Look at the Personal Social Services*. Policy Studies Institute, discussion paper no. 4, February 1981.
3 Speck, P. W., *Loss and Grief in Medicine*. Baillière Tindall 1978.
4 Marris, P., *Loss and Change*. Routledge & Kegan Paul 1974.
5 Oliver, M., *New Society,* 6 August 1981.
6 Bloom, S. W., *The Doctor and his Patient* (Collier-Macmillan and New York, The Free Press 1965), p. 41.
7 Parker, R. A., Inaugural Lecture, the University of Bristol, 1970.
8 Shepherd, A., 'One body', in Hunt, P. (ed.), *Stigma: The Experience of Disability* (G. Chapman 1966), p. 64.

TEN

Some professional implications of helping

Help is not given in a vacuum. It is given to a particular person and family in particular circumstances. The helper has some opportunities but at the same time is exposed to pressures and constraints. This has been called the environment of helping.[1] In this chapter I discuss aspects of this environment which may aid or hinder pastoral care with disabled people and their families.

Values and goals

To offer help to a person in a particular situation is to offer to change that situation in some way. So the helper must be clear about the purpose of the help and the direction of the change. What is the good that the helper is trying to achieve? To define a good involves a system of values. But whose values system does the helper accept as the basis for helping? His or her own, that of the person being helped, or that of the person's family? Or the official values of the Church of which the helper is a member even if his or her own values differ? There may be four different sets of values, four different ideas about the good to be achieved. This conflict of values, these differences in the ideas about the good to be achieved, may put the helper under considerable pressure; and this may be intensified if colleagues of other professions have still different values and aims.

Mrs Northwood was in her middle twenties and became an ardent convert when she married a Roman Catholic. When her first baby, a boy, was born he was found to be suffering from a rare, disabling disease which is hereditary. The genes which result in the development of the disease are carried by the mother. She does not suffer from the disease, but she passes the genes on to her children. Her daughters become carriers like herself and her sons suffer from the disease. This was explained to Mr and Mrs Northwood by the genetic counsellor, who expressed his own opinion and advised them not to have any more children. This counsellor used his own values and also made a definite recommendation. Mr and Mrs Northwood agreed with him and thought that they might adopt a child when they had become used to caring for their severely disabled son.

However, they refused advice about contraception, Mrs Northwood being quite vehement about it. They used the safe-period method of contraception but Mrs Northwood again became pregnant. Her general practitioner, the obstetrician and paediatrician all recommended that her pregnancy should be terminated and that she should be sterilized at the same time. Mr Northwood opted out of all discussions but agreed to accept his wife's decision — an attitude which made Mrs Northwood feel very isolated. She was distressed at the thought of losing 'her' baby and also because she equated sterilization with loss of femininity and sexual attractiveness. She talked over these aspects of her difficulty with me. Eventually she was able to put into words her recognition of the fact that the purpose of an abortion was to prevent the possible birth of a second disabled son whom she felt she could not cope with, or the birth of another carrier like herself. This aspect of her problem was made more difficult by her feelings of guilt that she, as a carrier, was responsible for the disability of her son. She recognized that sterilization would enable her to have relaxed sexual relations with her husband without any fear of pregnancy, but she felt that she did not deserve this; she was too guilty. We discussed her ambivalence; and, on balance, she wanted surgery. However, as a devout Roman Catholic, she thought it was wrong.

Mrs Northwood put the religious aspects of her problem to the Roman Catholic chaplain at the hospital. He was a newly ordained priest, recently appointed to the hospital, and his inexperience added to his dilemma. He considered that abortion and sterilization were lesser evils than the birth of severely disabled babies. He discussed his problem with the experienced Anglican chaplain in the hospital. I do not know in what way the priest resolved the conflict between the values of the Roman Catholic Church and his own, which he shared with the genetic counsellor and the other medical staff, but he encouraged Mrs Northwood to have surgery and he supported her in the months that followed.

Individual help and social change

It is probable that the majority of people in the helping professions see their task as being to help individual disabled people and their families with their problems, taking into account the social circumstances and using all the resources available. But is this sufficient? If the needs of a group of disabled people cannot be met under existing circumstances, has the helper the responsibility to extend his or her help to effecting changes in society so that the needs can be met? This question becomes more important, not less, in a time of economic difficulty.

It is clear that many of the difficulties of disabled people are intensified by the attitudes held by members of the public and that other problems arise directly from these attitudes. Indeed members of all the helping professions have a big responsibility to help to change attitudes; and they are well placed for their own attitudes to filter outwards to influence all those with whom they come in contact.

But if attitudes do not change quickly enough so that, for example, there is a long delay in new legislation for the benefit of disabled people, have clergy and other professional workers the responsibility of helping in more active ways? By writing to the local Member of Parliament or to the press? What is the limit of professional responsibility, and is this limit different from that of volunteers co-operating with professionals? If professional helpers consider that these activities should be included in the methods they use to help disabled people, would they expect to engage in them on their own or with a group of like-minded people? De Juvenel pointed out that a 'more powerful other', in this case an organization, could effect changes in a future that is controlling for an individual. For this reason, the Spastics Society recently organized a very peaceful demonstration in Trafalgar Square, London, to press for better provisions for ante- and post-natal care to reduce the risk of disability in newborn babies. Thousands of signatures were obtained and taken to Downing Street. If professional people take part in such activities, does it affect their relationship with other members of their own profession or with their employing organization of which they are accredited members?

Members of the caring professions must decide for themselves how they can best help disabled people. Their decision will be influenced by their perception of their professional task and by their ability to give individual help, or help to effect social change, or both. For my part, I have given individual help to disabled people and their families. As a member of a team consisting of different professions and, later, as a university teacher, I tried to influence the attitudes of colleagues and students; and to influence wider groups by publishing my research findings and other articles and by speaking at conferences. If I am described as a crusader, then my motivation and sense of direction are firmly based on my professional experience complemented by research.

Professional co-operation

Four of the many professions most closely concerned with the care of disabled people are clergy, doctors, nurses and social workers. The working relationships between these four professions are influenced by several factors which include their different origins, their different historical development and their different professional education.

A professional education imparts facts and the skills to apply them in methods of practice; it influences students' attitudes and values and their philosophic world-view. In turn, these influence the aims of the care which the qualified professional gives. They also have a marked effect on the kind of relationships which the professional establishes with the people he or she sets out to help and with members of other helping professions.

If the policies of care which I recommended in the previous chapter are to be implemented, members of the helping professions need a body of knowledge, and the skills to implement it, which are not as yet widely included in the educational curriculum of all the professions. The policies call for the establishment of a kind of relationship with disabled people and their families which is not consistent with that traditionally adopted by some professions. What may be required is an increased understanding of individual and social psychology, with emphasis on interpersonal relationships and some familiarity with the dynamics of the behaviour of people in small groups. There may therefore be a need for some changes in basic professional education and for opportunities for further study after qualifying.

At present, some members of each of the four professions do not correctly understand the aims of the other professions or the methods that they use to achieve those aims. This frequently leads to inaccurate stereotyping and the growth of prejudice, which in turn may give rise to professional jealousy. Some years ago the Institute of Religion and Medicine had a poster showing a man lying spread-eagled on a bed, while one member of each of these four professions pulls hard, one to each of the man's four limbs. The poster was entitled 'Professional Co-operation?'.

Such competition is not necessary. Each profession has its own characteristic area of expertise which is not possessed by the other three. The professions are complementary and a disabled person may need the specialist skills of all four. In the whole person model there are different aspects of a person: because each of the professions is concerned with caring for the whole person, each profession is now starting to acquire at least an elementary knowledge of part of the area of expertise of the other three professions. (This is represented in Figure 3 on page 134.) If the area of expertise of a profession is represented by a circle, the centre of the circle represents the focus of interest of that profession, the professional orientation. However, for example, the areas of expertise of a doctor and a nurse are different but there is some overlap—there is an area of knowledge and some skills which they have in common (represented by the shaded area in Figure 3). But even in the areas of overlap, the professional orientation of the two professions remains distinct. This concept of a specialist area of expertise with a characteristic orientation, even in the areas of overlap with another profession, can be applied to each of the four professions in relation to one another.

It is mainly because there are these areas of overlap that

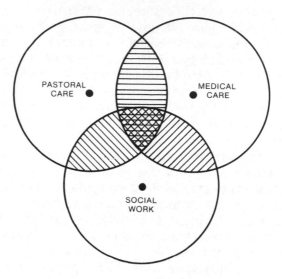

Figure 3 Areas of professional expertise

professional jealousy may occur: some members of the
professions need to defend their boundaries against intruders.
But these areas of overlap offer the opportunity for
professional co-operation; common ground as a starting point
for professional communication; the opportunity for a
discussion of different professional goals, values and methods
of working.

Communication and confidentiality

Co-operation between the professions and with disabled
people and their families is often hindered by difficulties of
communication. Each professional group uses its special
concepts and professional vocabulary, which are related to a
special way of perceiving and analysing situations: all this
affects the type of relationship which the professional
members establish with each other and with the people they
are helping.

In an earlier article,[2] I showed in what ways the practice of
modern scientific medicine may put strains on the doctor -
patient relationship and remove some of the personal content

from clinical practice. By contrast, social casework is personal—it is focused on the individual and requires some degree of personal involvement by the social worker with the disabled person. The relationship between the social worker and the client is private not public, i.e. it cannot be exactly repeated under the same circumstances by any other similarly trained worker. (This is in contrast to the public relationship in which such repetition is possible.) I suggest that the relationship between a clergyman and a disabled person is also private in this sense. Why then should frictions arise between clergy and social workers (perhaps more frequently than between clergy and doctors or nurses) when they establish the same kind of relationship with people?

Perhaps one reason is the difference in the origins of the two professions and their different historical development. One sympathetic analysis of the role of the clergy[3] says:

> In the past, the role of the parson was clear: the pastor with the cure [i.e. care] of souls, the representative of a compassionate Church whose responsibility it was to care for the poor and destitute, to educate children and comfort those who suffered; a leader among others of the local community; and the president of long-established organizations to help in all this. Now the wider community assumes responsibility for the social services and for education; advances in psychology and psychiatry have created other specialists in human problems of maladjustment, of guilt and despair; and a formerly stable parish population has made way for one of constant mobility with many interacting groups of which the focus is not the parish church.

It is against this background that the author continues: 'Status, role, identity: all these are alleged to be unclear in the minds of the clergy themselves, of the laity and of uncommitted society.'

Concurrently, the social work profession has changed. During the 1950s and 1960s, the one-to-one casework relationship was the principal method of social work: now it is but one of several methods, which include social work with groups of clients together and also community work with its strong element of social change. Furthermore, most social workers are now employed by local government so that their practice is influenced by the policy of the local Social Services Committee: they have an increasing number of statutory duties to perform in relation to children at risk and to people who offend against the law. They themselves may experience conflicts between their perception of their professional task and the policy of their employers, and with their statutory duties.

Bring members of these two professions together, and it is not surprising that neither is clear as to the functions of the other, or that sometimes both may become defensive and try to guard against encroachments by the other.

A subject which causes anxiety to both professions is that of confidentiality of information. Doctors and social workers sometimes withhold relevant information which the other needs because neither trusts the other to use it properly: and the same suspicion and practice may sometimes apply to clergy and social workers.

What is the way out of these difficulties when they arise? I suggest that they can best be tackled at the local level, with clergy and social workers getting to know each other as people, not as representatives of two large organizations who contact each other by telephone—if at all. The opportunity then arises for a discussion of values and goals and for a clarification of the areas of professional overlap, leading to a greater understanding of each other's complementary skills. This endeavour requires some humility on the part of both, but it can lead to professional trust. When trust has been established, there is the possibility of sharing information, with the disabled person's consent. When the two professions can communicate and share relevant information; the way is open for their co-operation to the benefit of the disabled people and their families.

References

1 I am indebted to Professor R. A. Parker for the concept of the environment of care.

2 Garrad, J., 'On the margin of the impossible', in *Journal of Medical Social Work*. Vol. 19, (1966), p. 84. A discussion of professional communication.

3 Howell-Thomas, D., *Mutual Understanding. The Social Services and Christian Belief.* Church Information Office 1974.

ELEVEN

Our time is now

Disabled people and the churches

In this chapter the emphasis is on the relationship between disabled people and members of church congregations, those who carry the awesome responsibility of being the people of God. In the hope that it may be of help to them when deciding how to fulfil their responsibilities in their local situation, we shall look at the principles underlying a number of schemes which have been working well for some years.

The existence of such schemes does not underestimate the value of the pastoral caring by individuals to others in their congregation or in the wider community, but sometimes the needs are too complex, or too numerous, to be met by individual effort alone. Then the service given by a group of people in the name of their whole congregation must be co-ordinated if it is to be effective: and the whole congregation must give this group its active and prayerful support. This support or lack of it is revealed in small but telling ways. In some congregations disabled people who, for example, use a wheelchair or who have tremors of the head or arms, are encouraged to sit at the back of the church in order not to inconvenience or distract able-bodied worshippers. This denies them equality and thus negates the positive attitudes of those members who have brought them to the church in their cars. When a church has chairs rather than pews, a chair may be removed to make space for the wheelchair, so that the disabled person is not placed conspicuously in the aisle but can sit in the row with his or her family or friends.

The form of service given by a whole congregation and by a special group in a Good Neighbour Scheme may be of several kinds. It may be to individual disabled people and their families, or to a group of disabled people, or to the community of which the disabled people are a part. The help may be given through the personal resources of the church, by using the time, skills and special knowledge of church members; or it may be through the use of its capital resources such as buildings, land or money; or by the two in combination.

Good neighbour schemes

Organization

Detailed literature is available for congregations thinking of starting such a scheme,[1] so what follows is a brief outline with emphasis on aspects that are of importance in relation to disabled people.

The principle is that a congregation takes a decision overtly to participate in pastoral care jointly with the clergy: they do so through their active support of a group of church members who offer their time, skills and knowledge to complement those of the clergy in a joint partnership. Usually a sub-committee of the Parochial Church Council or Church Board forms the executive committee, consisting of representatives of the principal committee and of volunteer helpers. Sometimes a panel of advisers or consultants is available to give specialist information or advice when needed: they may include a member of the clergy, a general practitioner, a social worker, a lawyer. At times these advisers are specialist members of the executive committee.

In some schemes a member of the clergy is the chairman. This may have the disadvantage that the scheme comes under his direction and the volunteers implement his programmes. When a member of the laity is chairman with the clergyman as a member of the committee, the responsibility of the laity in pastoral care is clear.

Recruitment of volunteers

The method of recruitment of helpers is important. In some schemes, the executive committee accepts all volunteers, even if some are known to be unsuitable because of their attitudes or temperament. In other schemes, the service of such volunteers is declined: when the chairman is a member of the laity, any resentment arising from this decision is deflected from the clergy. Sometimes, an otherwise unsuitable person may be included in the scheme as a back-up person to a front-line volunteer. For example, if a volunteer is working closely with disabled people and brings them to church by car, the back-up person can have the responsibility of ensuring in advance that their places are available in the church. It is an advantage if each volunteer discusses with the committee what his or her particular contribution can be, so that the appropriate person may be called on when a need arises.

There is no reason why all helpers should be able-bodied. People's different physical impairments make them disabled in different ways while they are able in other ways. The abilities of disabled people should be as fully used in the life of the congregation as those of physically able-bodied members. It is an example of the reciprocity of service in a shared enterprise. A disabled woman, whose mobility was severely limited, received help with her shopping from a member of a Good Neighbour Scheme; she herself was a member and helped a semi-literate man in the congregation to learn to read when he came regularly to her flat for reading practice. She also did the mending for a blind woman whose husband delivered and collected the articles.

Induction of volunteers. Some training or induction of volunteers is desirable. This emphasizes the responsibility which they are undertaking, positively increases the relevance of their help and reduces the chance of errors or infelicities. The induction programme should emphasize the importance of confidentiality, and should include both factual and attitudinal information. The sessions are usually discussion-type meetings, led by the clergy and specialist advisers. Some churches commission their volunteers during public worship, which thus involves the whole congregation, and in the induction programme they include instruction on the theology of Christian service and neighbourliness.

Support and supervision of volunteers. The volunteers need support because they will certainly encounter situations of unhappiness or deep distress among some disabled people, and they may need help to cope with their own emotions. The ready availability of a committee member or an adviser is important if the volunteer's need is urgent. Regular, say three-monthly, meetings of the volunteers with the committee and one or more of the advisers provide the opportunity for discussion of the ethical or social problems encountered; for discussion of worrying aspects of disability itself; or other subjects of common concern to all volunteers. It is helpful if every six months the focus of the meeting is a talk, followed by discussion, on a relevant topic by a specialist or a panel. This increases the volunteers' knowledge and, if the meeting is open to all members of the congregation, it is an opportunity for them to learn more about the complexities of pastoral care. In one church, there was a discussion about disabled people in the community and all the panel of speakers were disabled. The impact of this meeting was very great and considerably altered the attitudes of several church members.

Volunteers may be helping in situations of considerable delicacy, so that supervision as well as support is necessary. In some schemes volunteers are required to make a regular report, monthly or quarterly, written on a special form, so that the committee can monitor the help given: in other schemes verbal reports are given more frequently. The advantages of a written report are that there is a record in case of subsequent difficulty; it serves to underline the necessity for confidentiality and clearly distinguishes the reporting-back from gossip; and it emphasizes the volunteers' responsibility in pastoral care.

Area or road stewards

Some schemes have stewards whose responsibility it is to get to know all the residents in their road or area; to let them know that help is available if they need it; and to try to meet a need when it arises and when they are asked for help. People at risk are offered a card to be put in their window when they need help. In one scheme the card reads, 'HELP. Please telephone —', giving the telephone numbers of the chairman and secretary. If a passerby sees the card before the road steward does, then the committee is alerted. The chairman told me that she frequently receives telephone calls which start 'Are you HELP?' In some schemes the stewards have a card in their windows bearing the sign of the fish, sometimes with the name of the scheme and a central telephone number.

Requests for service

Information about people needing help is usually given to the secretary or other nominated member of the committee, who then asks a volunteer with the appropriate abilities to accept the task. The information may be given by the clergy who have come across a need in the course of their pastoral work which they think could be best met by a member of the laity; by road stewards; by other volunteers; or by general practitioners and social workers. Less frequently, the people in need make a direct approach.

Discreet publicity is therefore necessary. A letter to all general practitioners in the area and to the local Social Services Department is a useful beginning, in conjunction with a notice in the local library, town hall, on the church noticeboard and in the parish magazine.

Service in secular organizations

Where there is a flourishing secular voluntary organization, such as a local Council of Social Service, which runs a Good Neighbour Scheme, it is usually undesirable for a church to start a new scheme. This usually duplicates a service and there is a big risk that the church's scheme may not be as effective, because volunteers from different churches in the area are usually active members of the existing scheme and cannot effectively work in two schemes. In these circumstances, the constructive policy is for a church actively to support the existing secular scheme, by encouraging more members of the congregation to become volunteers in it. In this way, they increase the effective service to the community by enlarging the number of helpers, and, more important, they introduce another element in the range of care available—the pastoral component of care in and by the community. By their attitudes, and by the fact of their church affiliation and by their actions, they bear witness to their faith and to the source of their motivation.

Service in groups

Use of personal resources. The implication of all this may be
that the help is given on a one-to-one basis. This is not always
so. Some people's needs may be best met in groups,
particularly in groups of young people. Young people who are
members of a Good Neighbour Scheme, or any motivated
young people, can ensure that disabled people of the same
ages are welcomed as equals into the church's activities for
young people — whether the disabled people are church
members or not. Because the number of young disabled
people is small, local churches sometimes co-operate in this
aspect of service.

In one parish in the Netherlands, the young people set up a
joint group with severely disabled young people living in a
residential home in the district. It started as a secular
discussion group, but when subjects such as 'What is the
motivation for life?' were debated, all the members realized
that there is a theological aspect to most questions. They
moved on to discussing what were the difficulties in their
own lives, and in what ways and to what extent they could
help each other: not just the able-bodied people helping the
disabled people, but being helped by them. This resulted in
increased mutual understanding of each other's lives and in
mutual dependence.

Use of personal and capital resources. In a further example
from the Netherlands, all the congregations of one Protestant
denomination contributed to build and run a residential
holiday home for people (of any denomination or none) who
are so severely disabled that they can only have a holiday in a
purpose-built home.

This use of capital resources is combined with personal
service. Members of a church congregation, or of a group of
neighbouring congregations, make up a mixed group of
disabled people and able-bodied volunteers. The volunteers
attend to the disabled people's physical needs throughout the
holiday week and help them to organize and take part in
individual and group activities. A volunteer doctor and nurse
are available to attend to their medical and nursing needs. All
these volunteers frequently take a week of their own holidays

in order to participate. The minister from the parish usually shares in the full programme, giving pastoral help to those who need it and conducting services for those who wish to attend. At the end of the week each volunteer (except the doctor and nurse) keeps in touch with the disabled person he or she has been helping during the week. This continuing relationship is recognized as being an important part of the disabled people's contact with the wider community.

In Britain, church halls are frequently made available for community activities, including those which involve disabled people. One church donated a piece of land, which was surplus to its requirements, to a voluntary organization for the building of a residential home.

Reconciliation

The principle underlying all these different kinds of service is the Christian ministry of reconciliation. Reconciliation aims at bringing together again those who have become separated: man separated from God; man separated from man; disabled people separated from able-bodied people. 'He has made the two one, and in his own body of flesh and blood has broken down the enmity that stood like a dividing wall between them . . . so as to create out of the two a single new humanity in himself, thereby making peace' (Eph. 2.14, 15).

The task of Christians is to identify aspects of society which lead to isolation and seek to show ways of rectifying them. In their contacts with people, the task of Christians is to help them move out of isolation into fellowship, and to foster and support these relationships.

In the course of this endeavour, volunteers from church congregations have to be careful fully to respect the integrity of the disabled person. To use the opportunity of service for direct evangelism is to abuse their position as helpers, by taking advantage of their relative power as helpers compared with the relative weakness of the recipients. Helpers must let their actions be their Christian witness. The deed and the word are both forms of witness, both forms of proclamation. They are both equally valuable but on some occasions the former may be more relevant than the latter. If, however, volunteers are asked by a disabled person or others about their motivation or particulars of their faith, then they are given the opportunity to speak about the gospel and have a responsibility to do so. When helpers are asked to explain their faith, it is important that they should do so without dogmatism and without alienating the person whom they are trying to help. This is particularly important in counselling because mutual respect is fundamental to the counselling relationship. In the context of Christian service in and to the community, the essential starting point is the mutual acceptance of the helper and the person as people, just as they are.

When the helper is offered the opportunity to speak as well as to act, I believe that he or she should place emphasis on the fact that God is God of all the world, even though the world is not whole but divided into factions which compete and war with each other. But because God was in Christ reconciling the world to himself, we have the Christian hope of reconciliation — horizontally and vertically — God and man, and man with man. Furthermore, we have been entrusted with this message of reconciliation. 'He has reconciled us men to himself through Christ, and he has enlisted us in this service of reconciliation' (2 Cor. 5. 18).

References

1 The following publications are recommended by the Social Policy Committee of the Board for Social Responsibility of the General Synod of the Church of England:

Action for Care. The Volunteer Centre 1981. This is a survey of Good Neighbour Schemes in England.

Volunteers in the Neighbourhood. The Volunteer Centre 1982. This gives guidance to those planning a neighbourhood-based project which aims to offer care of any kind.

The address of The Volunteer Centre is 29 Lower Kings Road, Berkhamsted, Herts HP4 2AB.

Epilogue

In the preceding chapters I have drawn attention explicitly and implicitly to questions which have a profound theological importance: issues of life and death and, in particular, the problem of suffering. However, important as they are, the theological aspects of these problems are not the focus of this book and it would not be appropriate to include a discussion of them here.

My concern is rather for a group of people who suffer, and whose suffering is sometimes caused or increased by the attitudes of the able-bodied people among whom they live. The principal focus of the book is on the relationship between disabled people and able-bodied people. I believe that pastoral care should be many-sided, involving help of many kinds, which includes influencing the attitudes of able-bodied people: and it should be concerned with the whole person in his family and social setting. I have also emphasized that the giver-receiver relationship is not desirable and that the keynote of care should be reciprocity. This conviction is based on social and psychological premises but, as a Christian laywoman, my thinking and practice are underpinned by what I believe to be the correct interpretation of reciprocal service and of the relationship between the Church and disabled people. There are three principal sources for this underpinning.

In the Rijksmuseum in Amsterdam there is an oil painting by a sixteenth-century artist known only as the Master of Alkmaar. It is a series of seven panels entitled 'The Seven Acts of Mercy' and it is based on Jesus' teaching about service as recorded in Matthew 25. It portrays, in vivid and homely scenes, villagers drawing a stranger into their family group, others alleviating the lot of prisoners, feeding the hungry, caring for sick and disabled people and so on. The panels show the variety of service which Jesus called for, and they

146

emphasize the universality of the different needs which a community is called upon to meet. In all communities there are those who are alienated; or who are sick or disabled; or who are hungry or destitute; or who are imprisoned — literally or in some prison created by social or psychological factors. The ordinariness of the people in the paintings emphasizes the fact that at one time we may be among those who offer care and at another time we may be the people in need. Simultaneously, the paintings illustrate the concept of the presence of Jesus in every person, so that service offered to our fellow-men is service to God.

To me, the story of the disciples on the Emmaus road, at whatever level it is read, offers the possibility of moments of illumination, or at least of greater insight, in the course of our daily lives; and these seminal experiences may come in unexpected circumstances. This calls for a balance, which is difficult to maintain, between humility and openness on the one hand, and professional and personal confidence on the other. For me this conceptual approach is figuratively held in my mind's eye in the form of a Rembrandt drawing in a private collection in London. This portrays the stranger between the two disciples outside their home in Emmaus at the moment when they invite him to stay. Later, during the evening meal, the guest becomes the host by assuming the host's function of breaking and blessing the bread.

The examples given in the Gospels of Jesus' own service to individuals show that he was involved with the whole person. He was concerned with a person's relationship with God; he was equally concerned with the person's physical and mental health; and with his incorporation into a fellowship of mutual trust and mutual caring.

It is these approaches which underlie my social and psychological approaches. A Quaker, writing on the transition from loneliness to fellowship, points out that both religion and psychology emphasize that 'the good life is a life of love, co-operation and participation.' He believes that in order to achieve this, men must again experience 'what it is to stand face to face with other men, what it is to belong together, to be bound in one fellowship, in brief to be rooted.'[1]

This need is experienced by able-bodied and disabled people alike, and each can contribute to the self-realization and rootedness of the other. A ministry of clergy and lay people is incomplete without the ministry of disabled people in a wider expression of the diverse gifts of the same Spirit; an expression which may be given by some people who are not professing Christians.

Laurens van der Post referred in an essay to the well-known lines of John Donne, the Elizabethan poet: 'No man is an island, entire of itself; every man is a piece of the continent, a part of the main.' Van der Post continued:

> What he says moves me very much, but it does not carry me far enough because I feel that in a very, very deep sense we are each charged to be an island, within our innermost self. An island is a symbol of what is truly individual and unique. . . . My own view is that every man unto himself is an island, joined to other islands by the great sea of belonging, this vast ocean of creation in which every night and day we take part.[2]

In relation to the Church, can we say that disabled people are joined to other people by 'the great sea of belonging'?

About ten years ago, the World Council of Churches' Commission on Faith and Order examined the theme 'The Unity of the Church and the Unity of Mankind'. The division between able-bodied people and disabled people became evident, cutting across the life of all churches in every country, and found in each local situation. The report of the Fifth Assembly of the World Council of Churches in Nairobi in 1975 stated that disabled people 'are treated as the weak to be served rather than as fully committed, integral members of the Body of Christ and the human family; the specific contribution which they have to give is ignored.'[3]

Dr Lesslie Newbigin has recently argued that a congregation without the active participation of disabled people is itself disabled:

> To be faithful to the Gospel, the Church must be the place both of the faith that rebels and of the faith that accepts; and it cannot be this unless the handicapped are, and are seen to be, an integral and indispensable part of its life. This is an insight which is urgently needed at a time when

the dominant theological currents have been towards its role as liberator, healer and champion of justice. The handicapped, the oppressed, the deprived are utterly indispensable to the Church's authentic life, not simply as those on behalf of whom the Church is called to labour in healing and in action for justice, but as those who *now,* as the deprived and handicapped within the membership of the Church, have a part to play, and a witness to give without which the Church will simply not be fully Christian.'

Dr Newbigin further argues that the part and witness of disabled people include what they can teach of 'faithful courage' in overcoming 'appalling obstacles'; and what they can teach of 'faithful obedience' in working out their discipleship within the unalterable limits of their physical impairments. Without this witness, the witness of the Church is incomplete in the real world in which men and women and children suffer.

For it is only when the witness of the handicapped is an integral part of the witness of the whole Church, that this witness is true to the Gospel of the Crucified who is risen, the risen Lord who is the Crucified. Only with this witness as part of its total message does the Church's message measure up to the heights and depths of the human situation.[4]

References

1 Aarek, W., *From Loneliness to Fellowship.* Allen & Unwin 1954. A study in psychology and Quakerism.
2 van der Post, L., *Religion and the Renewal of Man and his Societies.* Westminster Pastoral Foundation Booklet 1979.
3 Paton, D. M. (ed.), *Breaking Barriers.* Nairobi, World Council of Churches, 1975.
4 Newbigin, L., 'Not whole without the handicapped' in Müller-Fahrenholz, G. (ed.), *Partners in Life: The Handicapped and the Church.* Faith and Order Paper 89, 2nd ed. Geneva, World Council of Churches, 1981.

Thank God our time is now when wrong
Comes up to face us everywhere,
Never to leave us till we take
The longest stride of soul men ever took.

CHRISTOPHER FRY

Index

able-bodied people, a preliminary
definition 1-5
abortion 95ff, 130-1
access to and egress from buildings
41-2, 87, 121-2, 138
acquired disability: gradual onset 12;
sudden onset 13; religious and
philosophical questions 100-1
adolescence 47-8, 68-9
aggression, verbal 22-8, 53-60
ambivalence in attitude: to parents
53; to severely disabled babies
96-7
amputation 10, 15: as image of
bereavement 69-71
angina pectoris 19
anxiety 54-60, 119: before major
surgery 67; see also emotional
disturbance, fear, worry
aphasia 18-19
Aquinas, Thomas 90
arthritic diseases 16-17, 32, 87,
105-6
arthritic impairment 30
aspects of the whole person 71-5
asthma 16, 58
'at risk' 123-4
attitude 1-5, 22-39: of able-bodied to
disabled people 40-1, 122; of
church members to disabled
people 138; of disabled people to
doctors 23-4; to life 104, 120-1; of
parents and able-bodied people
towards sexuality of disabled
people 47-8; religious attitude 104
attitudes, changing 131

bereavement 69-71, 101-2, 108-17;
bereaved relatives 108-17 see also
crisis
'bereavement of the dying' 112

Berwick, Lin 20n
Bible verses referred to in the text: 1
Samuel 16.7 1; Proverbs
13.12 89; Matthew 25 146; Mark
12.30 63; Luke 10.25 120; Acts
20.35 80; 2 Corinthians 5.18 145
blame see guilt
Blau, P. M. 80
blindness 49, 93, 124
blood donors 84
body, mind and spirit as elements of
man 63
body-image see self-image
brain: congenital abnormalities 11;
tumour 11
bronchitis, chronic 2-4, 15-17, 87

cardio-vascular disease 19
caring teams 126-8
cases: anon (broken neck) 100; the
Andrews family (spastic child)
34-6; Angie (cerebral palsy) 47,
93; Mrs Kitty Carpenter
(locomotor and internal
impairment) 103-4, 107n, 109-10,
114; Miss Elliott and Miss
Bradford (Good Neighbour
Scheme) 85; Mr Green (stroke) 40;
Mary Hamilton (diabetes mellitus)
7-10, 12, 15, 56, 68, 72-3, 123-4;
the James family (dependence
patterns) 30-4, 36, 68, 101; Mr
Peter King (terminal illness)
111-12; Mrs Northwood (bore
child with hereditary disablement)
129-30; Mrs Norwich (arthritis)
40; Mr O'Reilly (paraplegia,
incontinence, impotence) 26-30,
56, 63, 70, 118; Mr Roberts (bone
disease and generalized muscle
weakness) 22-6, 29-30, 56, 66, 70,

151

58-9; in physically disabled adults 57, 71; in physically disabled children 58; in the newly disabled 28, 56, 63-9
emotional functioning *see* emotional disturbance, mental health
emotional withdrawal 66-7
ending life, hastening death 97-100
engagement 93-4: Spastics Society residential courses for engaged couples 93-4
environment, influence of and influence on disabled people 33-9
'environment of helping' 129
epilepsy 16
equilibrium 75, 118
essential activities of daily life 36, 80-1: analysed 13-14
ethical questions 92-100
euthanasia 97-100

faith in God 104
Family Assessment Centres 29, 34, 124
family life-cycle 30-3, 42
fear: of blindness 73; of contact with disabled people 41, 43-4; of the future 78; *see also* anxiety, emotional disturbance, worry
fellowship 84
friendship and companionship 42, 44-5, 93
Fry, Christopher *xii,* 150
funerals 115-16
Fuller, R., reviewer in *Listener* 37-8
future, dominating 86
future, masterable 86

Gibbs, Kristine 20n, 102, 104-5
Giddings, R. 37-8
gift-relationships 84
giving 83-6
'Go-between-God' 103
goals of care 129-31
God 92-107 *passim,* 109; a loving Creator 104-7; the people of God 138
Good Neighbour Schemes 84-5, 114, 127; extended description of 138-44
grief: as 'work' 65, 67-9; chronic, 70
grieving and helping 114-17
Guardian: account of disabled woman (broken neck) 100; leading article on Mongol baby case of 1981 95
guilt feelings 100ff, 116

handicap: defined 13; and social life 13
head injuries leading to impairment 11
health defined 7; *see also* mental health
health and social care systems 36, 41, 82, 123-8 *passim*
heart: diseases in general 58; structural defects 11
heart attack 15-16, 19-20, 31
heart failure 17
heart transplants 96
help, helping 118-28: the church as helper 138-45; enlisting helpers 122; 'help' cards 141-2; long-term help 120-1; methods of helping 118-23; policies of care 123-8; service in secular organizations 142-3
hemiplegia 18
Hitler's policy of genocide 98, 105
Holy Spirit 103ff
home help (local authority) 81
hope 89-91, 113
hostility of disabled people 22-8, 53-6
housekeeper 81
housing facilities 93
Humanist Federation 43
humiliation 26-8, 53-6
Hunt, Paul 39n, 43-5, 82-3, 85, 88, 108

idealization, self- *see* self-image
identification 70
identity *see* self-image
impairment, physical, types described 10-11, 16-20; hereditary 95
impotence, sexual 26-9, 49, 63
incontinence 18-19, 26-9, 32
independence *see* dependence
Institute of Religion and Medicine 133
integration 94
integrity of disabled people, respect for 144-5 *see also* self-image
intellectualization of feelings 28
interdependence 79ff, 108
internal impairment 10

154 *Index*

International Year of Disabled
People (1981) 7, 13, 22
isolation, social 41-3, 84
issues of life and death 95-100

jealousy between disabled person
and helper 120
Jesus Christ 76, 105-6, 146-9; as
underpinning pastoral care 146-9;
as exemplifying service 146-9

kingdom of God 104
Kyle, Bill 76, 104

legislation of euthanasia 98
level of aspiration and attainment
22-39, 55
Lewis, C. S. 114-16
life enrichment 43-4, 112
life support after brain death 96
Lindemann, Erich 113
Listener, review by R. Fuller of R.
Gidding's autobiography, and
subsequent correspondence (1981)
37-8
locomotor impairment 10, 16, 53, 88
loneliness 40-5
long-term help 120-1
loss: bereavement 69-71, 109;
disability as loss 68-9; loss of
limbs or organs 10; *see also*
amputation
lung disease 2-4, 17, 87

Macquarrie, J. 89-90, 111-13, 117
malformation 10, 58; congenital 16
manipulation (emotional) of helper
by disabled person 120
marriage 45-51, ethical questions
93-4
marriage guidance 94
masturbation 48, 93
material problems of the disabled,
their effect on emotional health 60
mature dependence 79, 120
mental health: bereavement as a
hazard 71; definition by six
characteristics 56
mental illness 56-9; *see also* mental
health
mental retardation, mental
subnormality 11, 59
mind as an element of man 63
mobility 41-2: its effect on
emotional health 58, 60

models of disability, individual and
structural 122
Mongolism *see* Down's syndrome
moral basis of life 96
motivation 22-39 *passim,* 54
multiple impairment 11
multiple sclerosis 15
muscular dystrophy 43
myocardial infarction *see* heart
attack

Netherlands 42-3, 47, 98, 128
Newbigin, Lesslie 148-9
Niebuhr, Reinhold 90
numbers *see* statistics

obligation 80
occupational system 36

parenthood 94 *see also* children
parents of disabled children 47-8, 59,
92-3
paralysis 18-19, 32, 49, 53, 80
paranoia of disabled people 37-8
paraplegia 26
Parker, R. A. 136n
Parkes, Murray 69-71, 73-4, 116
pastoral care 92, 108-17, 118-28
perception, selective 29
philosophy of life 90-1, 100-7
physical contact: with disabled
people 120-1; with the dying 110
physiotherapy 23
Pinker, R. 81-2
pity 53
plan of God 105-6
planned dependence 79
policies of care 123-8
poliomyelitis 2, 10, 15, 64-5, 78-80,
109
political system 36
positive responses to crisis 65
Potter, Dennis 105-6
prayer 110
prediction and planning ahead:
predictive care 124-5
prejudice 23-5, 36-8
pressure groups 36
preventive care 123-4
professionals: co-operation 132-4;
competition 132-4; expertise 134
(diagram); responsibility 131
psychological impairment 11
pulmonary heart disease *see* heart
failure